THE JUDGES

A novel by

Eric J. Matluck

Also by Eric J. Matluck

Notes for a Eulogy

"A deftly crafted, psychologically complex, inherently fascinating, thoughtful and thought-provoking read throughout..."

MIDWEST BOOK REVIEW

The Judges by Eric J. Matluck

Published by Next Exit Press

ISBN: 979-8-9864253-0-6

Cover design and interior design by Paul Palmer-Edwards.

For my grandfathers

"*Don't wait for the last judgment; it takes place every day.*"

—Albert Camus

THE JUDGES

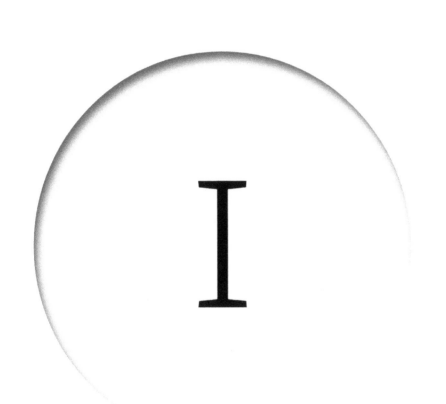

I

I'm looking at her picture—the famous one, the one that everybody knows—and thinking about her eyeglasses, wondering what was running through her mind when she bought them. Because you can learn a lot about a person if you know what she was thinking when she did something ordinary, like choosing a pair of frames. And in Mary's case—yes, Mary Sorabi—I have to wonder if she had any inkling of the way her life would turn out when she performed that one simple task. Did it make her happy? Sad? Or did she feel indifferent? And how long did she expect that feeling to last? Did she know how much happiness or what kind of sadness was going to follow?

For the few readers who don't know, Mary Sorabi won First Prize in the Graffman International Piano Competition in Philadelphia in 20—. And that year the prize may have been more meaningful than it had been the year before, because the previous year there was no First Prize awarded, just two Seconds. The judges felt that the two pianists who performed best, Knut Gigstadt and Jaap van der Sloewe, were equally good but not excellent enough to warrant a First Prize. That always struck me as poor. A competition is a relative judgment, as Mary would say, not a judgment against some defined goal. It's grading on a curve. One year's best may not be as good as the previous year's, but so what? What if one year's best is *better*? Do the judges go to the home of the previous First Prize winner and replace his or her gold medal with a silver one? Of course not.

And on the subject of eyeglasses, everyone knows that they were one of Mary's trademarks, because she wore a different pair every time she performed. On stage she never wore the same pair twice. Expensive? Not really, because the glass was clear; she didn't need them. And it wasn't because she liked the way they looked on her (this has been documented), it was because she thought it would make her stand out. At least to whoever was paying attention.

Oh, Mary. I remember you.

Naming a child Mary—simple, plain—is like writing a melody in C major: no sharps, no flats, just white keys. Ironic, of course, as Mary wasn't White. Her father, Vim Sorabi, was Indian, a pediatric surgeon, and her mother, Margaret Leung, was Chinese and a homemaker. She lived in the town where she grew up, Ardell, on the Jersey Shore, and often described it as "bleached" or "oversalted." She was referring to how drained of color it was. Most of the houses there had the chromatic neutrality of the people who lived in them, and the Sorabis were known as "the Asian family" or sometimes "the Asian clan," though there were only four of them—Mary had an older brother—but relatives visited often. Ardell was a "settled" community, founded, it was said, by descendants of the men who arrived on the Mayflower and wandered too far south. The only thing that was nurtured there was repetition. Or so Mary believed. But she never left because she didn't like change, either.

Anyway, the picture I'm looking at was taken when she was thirty, so just before she won the competition. It was posed, of course, but there was that familiar demure smile that had the quality of an afterthought. On stage and in the couple of interviews I've seen of her, to say nothing of our personal interactions, the smile never appeared spontaneously, only after a pause. Only after she gave thought to whatever was uttered or whatever occurred, and that made it more genuine. Even after her name was announced at the Academy of Music that Saturday night, she stood blank-faced before breaking into a smile and acknowledging the applause, which came at her, she later said, "like an avalanche. And who smiles during an avalanche?"

But first, of course, came the applause after her performance in the last round of the competition. Mary played three works from the twentieth century: Prokofiev's Piano Sonata No. 8 in B-Flat Major, Op. 84; Schoenberg's Suite for Piano, Op. 25; and Ravel's *Gaspard de la nuit*.

"Beyond daunting," said Miller Bruce, the man who won Second Prize that year, "and not at all attractive. At least not to me. What was she trying to prove?"

The music, Mary confessed, "was not 'written to please the ladies,'" a belittling phrase that someone had used in reference to Chopin's compositions, many of which were far from soothing or caressing or whatever it was "the ladies" were supposed to find pleasing. Mary loved music from the twentieth century.

"To me there's an exquisiteness to twentieth-century music that a lot of people don't hear," she said. "Don't get me wrong, I love a beautiful melody, but I hear beautiful melodies in handfuls of notes; they don't have to be expansive." Similar, one would suppose, to Twain's living on a good compliment for two months. "Most composers weren't great melodists. Only Schubert and Tchaikovsky come immediately to mind. Perhaps Chopin, Mendelssohn, Dvořák, and Grieg, but that's about it. And the piano is not essentially a melodic instrument. Its sound decays too quickly for a smooth flow of notes. The violin is melodic. So is the cello, whose range is the closest to that of the human voice, but not the piano."

Miller, on the other hand, had performed pieces by Brahms and Schumann, the two composers whom Mary held most dear, though she described his choice as "completely pleasant." And after Miller finished his recital with Schumann's *Symphonic Etudes*, Op. 13, the audience burst into riotous applause, but that could have been expected, Mary said, given the grandiloquence of the ending. "Sometimes I think that when a work ends loudly, the audience is applauding what you did with the last thirty seconds of it, but when it ends quietly, they're applauding your whole performance." Mary's last piece, Ravel's *Gaspard*, merely flutters away and almost takes one by surprise, but that final movement, "Scarbo," which was said to depict a menacing will-o'-the-wisp, is considered by many to be the single most difficult piece of piano music ever written, and much of the applause, Miller was sure, came simply because she attempted it.

Miller would later wonder if she chose that program to prove she had stamina because she was a woman. Mary would later wonder what kind of parents would name their son Miller Bruce.

But she knew what she was doing, not because she wanted to show off her technical prowess but because, she believed, she could find the lyricism that some people thought was hidden in, or missing from, "modern, difficult" music. And because she heard it, she could make her listeners hear it, too, allowing the music to go down as smoothly as lemon curd.

When the judges walked onto the stage, like three swollen doors that would no longer fit their frames, then smiled too brightly to show that this was *their* moment, to hell with whoever won or lost, Mary stopped thinking about herself and started thinking about them. Their names were Nicholas Meursault, Eldon Hilliard, and Arnold Druze; not a woman among them. And if their gait and appearance suggested social awkwardness—and isn't pride always tied to awkwardness?—one had to consider what they were doing and what they had done. They'd made a decision that they then had to sell to the audience. This wasn't a popularity contest, where the audience was polled to see who they liked best. So if the name of the First Prize winner received less applause than the names of the Second and Third Prize winners, they might have thought their decisions were wrong, which could have been especially damaging to their reputations, given what happened the previous year. Such is the life of a judge.

"Ladies and gentlemen," said Nicholas, first standing too close to the microphone on the lectern, then too far away, where he remained. "This was, perhaps, the hardest decision we've ever had to make."

Bullshit, Mary thought. No decision is ever difficult. What's difficult is rationalizing it, especially when you have to rationalize it to someone else. And whose benefit is that line for? The winner is going to think he or she didn't really win by that much, and the loser is going to kick himself or herself for having come so close but not quite making it. Losing by a single point is as ridiculous and cruel as being told by a doctor that he could have saved you had you seen him yesterday.

"But without any further ado," Nicholas said. Had he been talking while Mary's mind was wandering? She wasn't sure. "We're going to announce the names of the three top winners. First Third Prize, then Second Prize, then First Prize."

Mary swallowed so hard that the saliva wouldn't go down her throat, and she had to restrain herself from coughing. Coughing, she'd been told by her harmony professor at the Curtis Institute, was the sound any performer dreads most, to which Mary had replied, "Next to a piano that's out of tune and the nearest exit door being opened."

"The Third Prize, which includes a bronze medal, a cash award of twenty thousand dollars, US concert engagements and career management for the year subsequent to the announcement and presentation of this award, and a recording on the Double Eights label, goes to...Leonard Cohen."

Leonard, tall, thin, pale, and with dark brown hair so heavily slicked back that it looked as though the top of his head had been dipped in wax, rose, smiled, waved to the audience, and stepped onto the stage to receive his medal and certificate. Mary smiled, too; not to be supportive, not because she didn't hear her name mentioned, though both of those were true, but because she was thinking about Vladimir Horowitz's quote, "There are three kinds of pianists: Jewish pianists, gay pianists, and bad pianists." She wasn't sure how she felt about that, whether it was meant as a slight and a gibe or whether it showed how far minority representation had infiltrated the public consciousness, but she still thought it was funny.

"The Second Prize winner this year," Nicholas said, "and yes, this year we have only one," and there was not even muted laughter, which must have disappointed him, and he again enumerated what the award entailed, which was everything that was included with the Third Prize plus an additional ten thousand dollars and another year of concert engagements..."is Miller Bruce." Nicholas announced his name more quickly and comfortably than he'd announced Leonard's. There was no need for the gravitas and formality surrounding the mention of the Third Prize winner (the first name announced) or the First Prize winner (the last name announced). The Second Prize winner is always the middle child.

Miller, with his wide, flat face—pancake-like, as Mary would recall—and boxer's nose, walked up onto the stage and shook the judges' hands. Mary thought about his name. Perhaps his parents decided that, already having a last name that could have been a first name, they should give him a first name that could also be a last name, to create a sense of balance, however awkward it might sound. On the other hand, they might have feared he would be ostracized for having two first names. Maybe his father had been ostracized for that. And Mary wondered if, eventually, Miller would become a judge because others had judged him on his name.

"And finally. Finally," said Nicholas, "this year's First Prize...," and suddenly Mary didn't like the words "this year's," because they implied transience. Next year there would be somebody different, and possibly better, to receive that award, "...which includes a gold medal, a cash award of fifty thousand dollars, international concert tours and career management for the three years subsequent to the announcement and presentation of this prize...," and to Mary the judge's voice sounded like a record repeating itself, not entirely inappropriate under the circumstances, "and a recording on the Double Eights label, goes to..." and Mary was sure she couldn't feel her heart beating anymore... "Mary Sorabi."

"Whose parents are dead." She was surprised to hear herself say that, but that was the first thing that came to her mind when she heard her name announced and then recognized it as her own. Not because she wished they were there to share her happiness—she was too stunned to feel happy—but because the announcement made her feel exactly the way the doctor's and nurse's announcements had when she'd lost her father and mother. She'd been sitting in a hospital waiting room both times. When her father died a doctor came out and, four years later, when her mother died a nurse came out. And each said the same thing. "This year's First Prize goes to...." No. "I'm sorry, Ms. Sorabi; your father/mother is gone." And she felt a sense of collapse that ran quickly from her scalp down to her toes, but it wasn't the collapse she'd expected; it was a collapse into relief and then serenity because, in a sense, she was free. When you live in grave anticipation of a moment for long enough, you forget that you can ever feel differently. But then the moment comes and, because it's real, you accept it in a way you couldn't when it was only a fear or a hope, because there was nothing to grab onto then, nothing absolute to embrace. So again she realized that you can't prepare yourself for anything, because you never know how you're going to react until it happens.

Tears welled in her eyes, and what sounded like a roaring in her head turned out to be applause, and such applause as she'd never heard, at least not directed toward her. Seemingly she'd forgotten that she needed to step onto the stage, and even hoped she wouldn't attract too much attention by doing so, but then reminded herself that everyone was applauding her.

"Say something, Mary!" someone shouted.

But when she walked up to the judges, shook each of their hands, hugged them as tightly as she could, received her certificate, and then bowed her head so that Arnold could place the gold medal around her neck, she smiled, and said, "I'm going to leave it at 'thank you,'" and walked away. One of the truly great moments in her life that, she knew, she wasn't ready for, because she couldn't have been, and that she would appreciate only as time wore on, and possibly, though she hoped not, that she could think back to some day and say about it, "I was famous once."

Oddly, Mary would never remember exactly what the judges looked like, which was particularly surprising, as she'd considered studying with Eldon Hilliard at Curtis, but her mind must have been safely or distractedly removed enough to simply recall them as a corporate entity.

That night Mary sat alone in the bar of her hotel, the Saint Martin de Porres on Walnut Street, nursing a glass of tomato juice, her poison of choice, since she didn't drink alcohol, and thinking about how much she hated hotels that had "Saint" in their name. She believed them to be old and staid and sometimes blowsy, as that one was, but it was all that was available, and she didn't want to stay in the same hotel—the Warwick; equally old but less blowsy—that most of the other contestants were staying in, because she didn't want to be influenced by them in any way.

After eleven o'clock, in her room, undressed and lying in bed with the door locked, she called her three closest friends, Leila Meng, Lizzy Kelbick, and Julietta Han. They'd gone to New York University together, roomed with each other their last year there, and, after keeping in touch on and off for half a dozen years, ended up living within half an hour of each other. Leila was a French translator, Lizzy was an occupational therapist, and Julietta was an illustrator of children's books. Lizzy must have been out because Mary's call went directly into her voicemail, and Julietta didn't pick up her phone, but she rarely answered it on the weekends. Which was okay because it was Leila, her best friend, whom she wanted to talk to the most.

"Hello?"

"Hello, Leila?"

"Yes. Mary?"

"Leila, I have some news for you."

"Yes?"

"I won."

And after a pause, "You won what?"

Mary smiled. She knew that Leila knew what she was talking about, as any good friend would. "First Prize."

And after another pause, "In the piano competition?!"

"One and the same," Mary said. And then she heard the phone drop and Leila calling "Coming!" from what sounded like ten feet away, as though she'd tossed her phone across the room. "Oh my God! Mary. Mary! You're famous!"

And Mary laughed because that, she thought, must have been what mattered to Leila. It didn't to her. At least not then.

"Oh my God, Mary, I have so many questions for you, I don't know where to begin. When are you coming home?"

Mary stretched. "That's a good place to start. Monday."

"Monday," Leila said. "The day after tomorrow. All right. We'll have to celebrate."

Then Mary sighed, and Leila said, "Uh, I know what that means."

Mary let her head drop comfortably against the white faux-silk pillow-case and wished she had a glass of tomato juice with her. She liked having something to keep herself occupied with when she talked to people.

"I know," Leila said simply. "You'd rather not. That's okay."

"Thanks, Leila," Mary said, relieved. She yawned and stretched again. It wasn't that Mary didn't appreciate Leila's offer, it was that she didn't want to celebrate her win. A win was somebody else's opinion of what she did. Other people might be convinced of the quality of her work, but she rarely was, and celebrating it, or even talking about it, would only make her look harder to find fault with it. That was because Mary didn't trust other people's opinions, and there was nobody more critical of Mary than Mary was. Yes, constantly sitting in judgment of herself could be a chore, but she felt it was necessary so she would never disappoint her audience and, more importantly, never disappoint herself.

Still, she and Leila spoke well into the night.

The next morning, Sunday, Mary awoke at ten o'clock, which was unusually late for her. She'd planned to shower, eat her celebratory breakfast in the hotel's restaurant, Simone's, starting with either a large glass of orange juice or half a fresh grapefruit, both of which she enjoyed and both of which she knew were on the menu—Mary wasn't much given to spon-taneity, but from time to time, and especially after what had happened the night before, she liked indulging in it—then eggs Benedict, a side of hash browns, and a cup of black coffee. After that she would take a bus to the Philadelphia Museum of Art, a place she liked visiting when she was in the city, and where there was an exhibition of Bach manuscripts, and, time permitting, visit some smaller museums as well.

But she was confused when she woke up, as the first thing she noticed was that one of the buttons on the dark green rotary phone on her desk was lit. Somebody had called her. First she wondered why someone would call her on her room phone, especially as the only people who knew she was there—her friends and her agent, Mel Stargell—knew her cell number, and then she wondered why she hadn't been awakened by the phone ringing. Old telephones, she knew, rang loudly. But then, she'd slept through her alarm as well.

The call might have come from somebody at the front desk. It probably had, she thought, to let her know she'd missed her checkout time, but then she looked at the clock and realized that she hadn't, and then she reminded herself that she wasn't checking out until the next day. But no, it was a voice message from someone she'd never heard from.

The message sounded garbled. At first she thought that whoever left it—it was a man. Did he have a slight Southern accent? She couldn't tell—was eating while he was talking, but then she realized that his voice faded and then became clear again, so she figured he was calling from somewhere with poor cell service, assuming he was calling from a cell phone. Which he might not have been, because what he said, from what she could make out, was that he was a reporter for the *Philadelphia Inquirer*, who was working the night shift, and had just heard of her win in the Graffman Competition. So he wanted to interview her later that (Sunday) afternoon. If it was all right with her, he'd just knock on her door at four o'clock, she didn't need to call him back. Which was good, because he didn't leave a contact number. Then he hung up. Strange, Mary thought. What if it hadn't been all right with her? Would she simply ignore his knock? Leave her room beforehand? Alert hotel security? But intriguing, too. Mary had never been interviewed, and she liked the feeling of suddenly seeming famous, or at least a little familiar, and she always liked, and even needed, having something to look forward to. So four o'clock it was; she'd be back in her room by then. The interview structured her day more firmly, and then she was looking forward to it.

After breakfast—she chose the half grapefruit, which she thought was a little bitter—she took a bus to the art museum. Growing up on the shore, Mary never took a class trip to any museum in New York or Philadelphia, which were roughly equidistant from Ardell, because they were both too far away. Her mother, who grew up in what she called "the real Chinatown," in Manhattan—there are actually nine Chinatowns in New York, two of which are in Manhattan—used to love class trips to the Metropolitan Museum of Art, the Museum of Natural History, and the Brooklyn Museum, and she and Vim took Mary and her older brother Ken to museums in New York and Philadelphia every couple of months. But their parents also made it a point of taking them to smaller museums that celebrated their Chinese and Indian heritage, such as the Museum of Chinese in America, the Museum of the Asia Society, and the Rubin Museum of Art in New York, and the University of Pennsylvania Museum of Archaeology and Anthropology in Philadelphia, so the children, their mother said, "Wouldn't think that only White people contributed to culture." That said, some of the exhibits Mary saw showed how the Chinese and the Indians had been oppressed in America, about which her father said, "Still, most of them came to this country because things weren't any better at home."

"Sometimes people just follow what's familiar," Ken said.

"True," their father said. "Sometimes." But he said it questioningly, which made Ken feel like he wasn't being listened to. Then their father said, "Make up your own minds on how they were treated here, and how *you*'re treated here." Their father, who had spent his whole life in the United States, had come from a wealthy family and enjoyed the kind of privilege that most people don't, but forever remained intensely sympathetic to people who he knew were less fortunate, though he would stress that one couldn't generalize about how any defined group of people is treated. Mary's mother, whose upbringing was solidly middle-class, disagreed completely, but said very little, only agreeing that Mary and Ken needed to decide things for themselves.

All of which led to an uncomfortable situation one afternoon, when Mary was twelve. Her not-very-good friend from school, Bella Cerone, came to visit Mary's house for the first time. After being shown around, then sitting on Mary's bed, Bella turned to Mary and said flatly, "You're a racist."

"Why?" Mary asked.

"Because of the pictures on your walls. They're all Indian or Chinese. There's no White art here."

But Mary wasn't the type of girl, and would never become the type of woman, to defend herself in the most obvious way, such as by saying, "I didn't buy them; my parents did." She thought people deserved better. So instead she said, "I'm half Indian and half Chinese so I don't have 'White art' hanging in my house. But you're White, so how much Indian and Chinese art do you have hanging in yours?"

Upon entering Lenfest Hall at the Philadelphia Museum of Art, and even before she bought her admission ticket, Mary looked up and stared. She'd been to that museum dozens of times during the past twenty years, but never ceased to be thrilled by the sheer vastness of it, particularly the hall in which she stood and the exhibition halls. It said, in no uncertain terms, GREATNESS LAY HERE. Rooms in general, even big ones—and the houses in which she grew up and lived were spacious—weren't as large as the ones in the museum, so the hugeness of Lenfest Hall and the exhibition galleries showed her what could happen when one stretched something to its limits (though such limits could, arguably, never be reached) and made it extraordinary. It wasn't that Mary was impressed by space, per se; she was impressed by vast *indoor* space. Museums and concert halls thrilled her. Outdoor spaces didn't appeal to her at all. She preferred spaces created by humans and designed according to a plan over spaces created by nature, or by the Almighty, or whatever or whoever one believed in. Her living room looked out on the ocean, but that didn't impress her. And when she was ten and Ken was fourteen, their parents took them on a weeklong vacation to the Adirondacks, but she was bored. They stayed in Lake George and visited Lake Placid, Lake Champlain, Whiteface Mountain, Ausable Chasm, and other locations that were vast, but she remained steadfastly unimpressed. Nature was already extraordinary, in its way, so it wasn't putting on the same kind of show that human creations were. Though, if truth be told, nature didn't appeal to Mary primarily because she never liked being outside.

"That's odd," Leila said to her many years later. "You would think that someone who enjoys solitude as much as you do would love the great outdoors. The wide-open spaces."

To which Mary replied, "To enjoy solitude, there have to be people I'm getting away from. If there's no one there, and nothing around me but empty space, it actually feels claustrophobic."

"What about all the tourists?"

Mary shook her head and said, "After a while they become easy to ignore." She wouldn't say it to Leila, but she enjoyed being around people primarily for the pleasure of leaving them; of saying goodbye. To remind herself that yes, life was better when lived alone. *Frei aber froh*, Brahms had said. Free but happy. Which was, perhaps perversely, one of the reasons she so enjoyed being a performer.

For a few moments Mary thought about not looking at the paintings she usually looked at, in addition to any number of others, because her time was limited. She wanted to get back to the hotel by three-thirty to shower and change her clothes in preparation for the interview. She doubted that would give her enough time, but decided she'd rather be rushed than sit, wait, and feel anxious.

So she passed quickly through the galleries that held the dozen or so pictures she always stopped in front of when she came to that museum, and decided that people who love music were more fortunate than people who favored the visual arts. If one thought of live events—going to a concert, visiting a museum—as the most desirable way to experience art, one could listen to a good recording on good stereo equipment, and convince oneself, almost, that one were at a live performance. But looking at a painting in a book, a magazine, or online was nothing like seeing it in a museum. All of the subtlety and intricacy were gone. Which would explain why she always walked toward the same dozen or so paintings. Because she loved them and couldn't see them anywhere else.

When she'd first sat down with Mel, her agent, he'd asked her, "Would you rather know a lot about a few things or a little about a lot of things?"

And Mary said, "A lot about a few things."

Mel laced his fingers across his stomach and nodded. "Then you're going to have a limited repertoire," he said. "That's good. I like that."

And Mary said, "Really?! I don't. I'd rather know a lot about a lot of things but I don't remember your giving me that option."

The museum's special exhibit, the original manuscripts of Bach's six *Brandenburg Concertos*, were on display in the Dorrance galleries on the first floor. It wasn't clear what the curators meant by "original," since these were handwritten, not printed, manuscripts, and had many deletions, insertions, and corrections. Each concerto was displayed, in full score, in its own glass case that sat on six brass legs.

Bach had composed the concertos sometime before 1721, which was the year he presented them to his benefactor, the margrave of Brandenburg-Schwedt. Each was written for a different combination of instruments, which added variety to their sound—the mellow Sixth, Mary's favorite, used no violins—and, as Mary saw, their look on the page. They might not have been among Bach's greatest works, but they were certainly among his most popular, with many people familiar with their melodies without even realizing it.

Walking into the room in which the manuscripts were held, she was surprised to see how few people were there. It was a Sunday afternoon, traditionally one of the busiest times at a museum, but the scarcity of visitors disappointed her, and those who were looking at the manuscripts walked from one display case to another more quickly than Mary thought they should have. Maybe fewer people than Mary realized were interested in classical music. But then she had the happier thought that maybe fewer people than she realized were interested in museums. That made her laugh, and then she had a happier thought yet: it was only four weeks until Memorial Day weekend. The weather had turned comfortably warm, and not too humid, so maybe most people, unlike her, preferred being outside. In fact, she was sure that was it. But no. Most people simply couldn't read scores, so didn't spend overmuch time staring at them, but that never occurred to Mary.

Still, when she walked over to the first case and saw the manuscript of the First Concerto, her mood didn't merely brighten, she was transfixed. Other people might have seen just ink scrawled on paper, and it might well have been, but Bach, arguably the greatest musical genius who ever lived, and one of the greatest creators of any type, had written those scrawls himself. Reading the score, and, fancifully speaking, looking backward, she could almost imagine what must have been running through his mind when he wrote it. So many decisions: the choice of notes, the choice of instruments, the choice of tempi. But there it all was, and she felt even more transformed than she had the night before, because this was something she could relate to. She spent her life reading music, not winning awards.

She found herself spending longer staring at each manuscript than she thought she would and, for a moment, blamed herself for having looked at anything else first. She compared the handwriting among the six concertos. Was one more finely etched, more confidently written? Were the notes larger? Were there fewer cross-outs? For someone who was used to seeing only a finished, printed score, the changes that the composer made were unusually fascinating. And looking at what was deleted or changed, she found herself agreeing that, in each instance, Bach made the right choice, but who was she to say? To her what was right was what was familiar.

In all, she spent forty-five minutes studying them and coming back to certain concertos, before walking into an adjacent gallery that displayed instruments from Bach's time, some for which the concertos had been written. But she knew she had to leave, and stopped only for a few minutes in front of a single German harpsichord made of pine. Mary's father had once told her that never learning to play the harpsichord was the greatest regret of his life. And that day Mary thought that if that was his greatest regret, he'd lived a very enviable life.

Mary's father was her first piano teacher, and at one o'clock every Sunday afternoon, barring any interruptions, from the time Mary was eight until she was eleven, he would sit down next to her on the piano bench in their living room and prepare for her lesson. Rather than concentrate on technique, the way her subsequent teachers would, he thought it was important to develop her interest in music by explaining the history and background of each piece he introduced, and teach her about her own and music's place in the world, as Bartók was said to do with his son Peter.

Every Sunday, then, at one, her father would sit suddenly upright, after which Mary would copy his pose, and he would say, in his best stentorian voice, "Today's lesson will be called...," because each lesson had a title, as every lesson followed a plan. Then he would play a scale, rapidly and dramatically, in the key of whatever work they were about to discuss, and, suddenly dropping his voice and sounding almost apologetic, announce the name of the lesson. It always made her laugh.

One particular afternoon, when Mary was eleven, her lesson was called *Ethnic Diversity and the Baroque Keyboard Suite*. Her father said, "Keyboard suites were originally written to be played on the harpsichord, or clavichord, or virginal, or even the organ, whatever was around, but not on the piano, which hadn't been invented yet. That said, a lot of people like to play Baroque keyboard music on the modern piano, and since that's what we have, I'll explain it to you on this." He ran his right hand over the keyboard. "Harpsichords," he said, "usually have two keyboards, but we have only one to worry about."

Mary nodded, ever gracious.

"Now a suite, as you know, is a string of dances. But the Baroque keyboard suite was a string of *stylized* dances; which is to say, they were made to be played and listened to, not danced to."

"Why was that?" Mary asked.

Her father shook his head. "I don't know," he said. "What do you think?" He would always encourage Mary to express her opinions and never be afraid to say anything, even if he didn't agree with what she said or thought her answer was wrong. So sometimes, even when he did know the answer to something, though he didn't that time, he would say "I don't know," so she wouldn't feel intimidated that she couldn't explain herself correctly.

Mary looked around the room, then stared at the keyboard, lowered her head, and said, "Maybe because composers thought dancing was for the lower classes."

Her father laughed. "That's excellent. I'm pretty sure that the upper classes danced, too, but I like the way you think. Anyway, the basic keyboard suite consisted of five movements, and sometimes additional movements—dances—would be added to suit the composer's fancy, as you'll see. Because the piece we're going to learn about today, Bach's Fifth Partita for Harpsichord, in G Major, BWV 829, contains two minuets, but I'm getting ahead of myself. Anyway, the movements were a prelude, which was a good place to start, because it prefaced the actual dances that followed, and also presented the theme that would be varied in the succeeding movements." And he played the first movement of the partita, which Bach had labeled "Praeambulum." "Then came the allemande, the courante, the sarabande, and the gigue. Now here's what's so interesting. Each of the four dances came from a different country, so a different culture, so they sounded different. The allemande, as its name implies, was German, so it was a..." he hesitated... "serious, I don't want to say heavy, well–thought-out dance." He played several measures of that. "The courante came from France, so it was lighter, maybe frothier, more elegant, with more air in between the notes." Then he played her a little of that, so she could hear the difference.

She smiled and nodded.

"The sarabande was a Spanish dance, and as Spanish was said to be the most death-obsessed culture in Europe—so I've heard; please don't quote me on that—it's heavier, slower, and often sadder. As you can hear here." And he played a few measures of the sarabande from the partita. "And the suite would end, at least from Bach's time on, with a gigue, or what became a jig, which is a lively English dance." And he played a few measures of that.

"I thought England was gloomy," Mary said.

Her father smiled. "It is, sometimes, but, you know, the English love their sense of humor."

"And I guess they need it to combat the gloom," Mary said. Then they both laughed.

"Now here's the issue, sweet love." He always called her that when he wanted her to pay special attention to what he was saying. "With dances from four countries, in four styles, you would expect the Baroque keyboard suite to sound, well, multicultural, for lack of a better term. German, French, Spanish, and English. But it doesn't. The suites that Bach wrote, because he was German, sound German, and the suites that, say, François Couperin wrote, sound French. And so on."

"Maybe Bach and Couperin couldn't disguise who they were," Mary said.

Her father looked shocked for a moment, then leaned over and kissed her on the forehead. "Maybe they couldn't," he said. "Or maybe they didn't want to." Then he continued where he'd left off. "So the cultural and ethnic differences in the dances have been rubbed away; integrated, assimilated into the whole. And don't get me started on Bach's *French Suites*, which don't sound at all French, or his *English Suites*, which don't sound remotely English. But maybe Bach was ahead of his time," he said, then sighed a bit theatrically for her benefit. "I still remember when you could tell the nationality of an orchestra by the sound it produced. Yes, they all played the same instruments, and they played them in pretty much the same way, but the Czech Philharmonic sounded nothing like the Berlin Philharmonic, which sounded nothing like the Amsterdam Concertgebouw. Now? Not so much. And you could tell more easily—not always easily, but *more* easily—when a singer was singing in his or her native language by the way he or she pronounced the words. Now, to an extent, it all sounds the same."

"Is that good or bad?" Mary asked. "The assimilation."

Her father shook his head and laid his hands on his thighs. "I don't know, sweet love," he said, "and I don't know that it matters, in the great scheme of things, but when the time comes," and he never did explain what he meant by that, "you'll have to decide for yourself whether it's more important to become assimilated or to stand out. And whether it matters."

Her mother, who fortunately hadn't been listening, would often tell Mary that it always mattered; that she needed to take sides on everything, even if she didn't express them openly. Her father remained more equivocal.

By the following year such discussions had faded into memory, because Mary's parents hired Raul Romero, an ebullient Frenchman with a round face that always looked powdered—it wasn't—and waxed moustache, to give her professional piano lessons, and she liked to sit next to him because, she said, he smelled like her father. (As it turned out, they wore the same deodorant and bathed with the same soap. Neither ever wore cologne.) Raul lived five miles north of Ardell, in Sitters by the Sea, the town in which Leila would eventually settle. But there was none of the *serious* talk about other matters, cultural or even political, and Mary's father rarely mentioned them away from the piano. Which was one reason, Mary later explained, why music meant so much to her.

So at three o'clock that day after she won the competition, pleased with having allowed herself enough time to see what she wanted to see at the Philadelphia Museum of Art, and making a mental note to come back and take a closer look at the authentic instruments the next time she drove to Philadelphia, Mary left the museum and ran to catch a bus that would take her back to the hotel.

Once she got to her room, she breathed deeply, realized she was more anxious about her upcoming interview than she wanted to be, but meeting strangers always made her nervous, undressed, took a shower, redressed in the same clothes—she'd put them on fresh that morning—and sat on the bed, afraid to lean back because that might lull her to sleep, and waited for the interviewer to knock on her door. She wondered if a bell wouldn't have been better, but then decided that bells were too loud and knocks were more intimate.

And at exactly four o'clock a single knock came on Mary's door. She was in Room 818, which was quiet, as it was a fair distance from the elevator. If she weren't expecting it, she was sure she would have missed the knock or ignored it, thinking it was something else. And in the time it took her to realize what it was, there was only silence, no repeated knock and certainly no string of knocks. She was pretty sure that nobody had ever announced himself that way. So she walked slowly to the door, looked through the peephole, and saw a man standing there, but the peephole was dirty or maybe just worn, so she wasn't able to make out much about him. Still, she wanted to make sure that it wasn't a joke; somebody knocking once, then running away, or even a crowd of people wanting her autograph. She had to laugh.

When she opened the door she saw a man in his middle twenties, tall, thin, pale of complexion, not unlike Leonard Cohen, but with stringy, dark brown hair parted precisely in the middle, and a left front tooth that, as Mary would later describe it, turned shyly inward. He nodded, asked Mary if he could come in, and, after she said yes, introduced himself as a reporter for the *Philadelphia Inquirer*. Interestingly, he never gave his name, and she never asked him for it. Some people said that was because of the way she was raised: to never question a man, but she hadn't been raised that way at all. I think she just didn't care.

He was carrying a yellow legal pad, a black ballpoint pen, and a cassette recorder. Surely, Mary thought, contemporary reporters didn't use such outdated equipment, but she found it familiar so she found it reassuring, and when she asked him to sit in the red club chair that sat just to the right of the floor lamp that stood directly between her two narrow windows, she situated herself in the companion chair to the left.

"So anyway," he said, trying to sound acquisitive, "I've been asked to interview you about what happened last night."

Mary thought that sounded ominous.

He laughed, though more to himself than to her. "Your win, I mean. And then I'll get back to my office, and the interview will appear in the *Inquirer* in a couple of days. Sound good?" he asked, and smiled.

And Mary nodded stiffly and told him it sounded fine. As he talked, she noticed that he didn't have even a hint of a Southern accent, as she'd originally thought when he'd called, and at one point she wondered if he were the same man who'd left the message the night before. But eventually she convinced herself that yes, he was; the voice was the same. Or close enough. Maybe she just wanted to be interviewed more than she realized.

Anyway, he interviewed her for nearly four hours, stopping only because Mary said she was getting hungry, but they didn't pick up their conversation after dinner, as he'd originally told her they would, and when he left, he said that the interview would be published the following week in the *Inquirer*, no longer "in a couple of days." But the *Inquirer* never printed a word of it, and no such man was ever found working for the *Inquirer* or any other newspaper or magazine in Philadelphia. That said, excerpts from the interview did surface elsewhere and I, not surprisingly, have a copy of the complete, unedited transcript, portions of which I will share as appropriate, as they reflect on or illuminate certain parts of this story. But I must warn you, some of the questions were completely unprofessional and often downright ugly, so, taking everything into account, I have to wonder how "real" this interviewer was. That the interview was real, however, cannot be doubted because, as I said, I have an unedited transcript of it. Understand, though, that the excerpts will not appear chronologically, which is to say, their placement in the story will not follow the order in which the subjects were discussed.

Of note, the ordeal left Mary exhausted, though not unhappy, and she did break for dinner at Simone's that night, but she didn't enjoy it, because, having explained to the interviewer everything she wanted to, she felt curiously spent.

Mary left for home at eight o'clock the next morning, grabbing breakfast at a diner along the way.

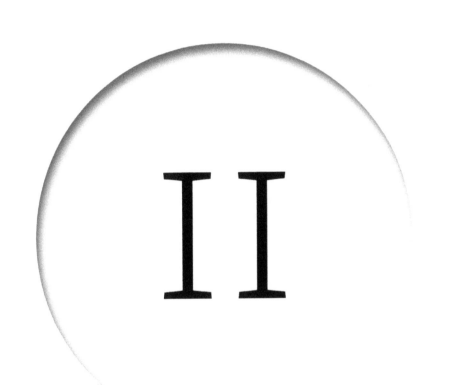

II

Mary lived by herself in a large shorefront house on Defoe Drive in Ardell. If you proceed north along Shore Road, which is Ardell's main street, more thickly tree-lined and heavily clustered with old shops and restaurants than most towns in that part of the state, you'll come, just before you reach Gillerson, to Defoe Drive, which forks sharply to the right. (Trying to turn left onto Defoe Drive, if you're heading south, is not easy, and there are no other roads that connect with it.) Then it runs for half a mile before ending in a cul-de-sac surrounded by four small white houses, all of which look the same. But the houses that face the road before you get to the cul-de-sac are large, elaborate, and unique, and Mary's stood midway down, on the right. It was number 111.

It had been built in the 1970s and was shaped like a V. You entered at the apex, where a shallow foyer gave way, two steps down, to a living room that occupied more than five hundred fifty square feet, so more space than the room in the hotel that Mary had just left. The room was square, which might mean that the house resembled a W more than a V, with the farthest corner facing the entrance. "Square rooms," Leila had told her, "are *so* 1970s," to which Mary responded that the house was just being true to its roots, before asking her kindly to shut up. The two far walls were mostly windows, from floor to ceiling, though reinforced to withstand the hurricanes that could hit, or so Mary was told, and dampen the noise from outside. They were draped in thick, dark gold brocade, behind which hung beige silk curtains. To the right sat her grand piano, in front of the right-hand window, and, facing the piano, but about ten feet back, was a large sofa with a floral pattern in embroidered chintz. In the far corner sat a recliner covered in gold velvet, and to the left of that, so in front of the left-hand window, a loveseat that matched the sofa. A mahogany cocktail table sat in front of the sofa, with end tables and crystal lamps on either side, and a drum table with a brass lamp sat next to the recliner. The walls were painted light gold and all the floors in the house, except the kitchen, dinette, and bathroom floors, were covered in tan high-pile carpeting, the perfect color for someone who lived on the shore and, especially, for someone who didn't entertain much. In the left wing of the house, as Mary liked to call it, were the dining room and, beyond it, the kitchen and dinette, and in the right wing were the bathroom and two bedrooms; the master bedroom to the left, which faced the ocean, and the guest bedroom to the right, which faced a yard.

Whenever Mary returned from anywhere, even if it was only a trip to the supermarket, she would walk carefully through every room, not to make sure that everything was exactly as she'd left it, that no one had come in and touched anything, but to remind herself how lucky she was to have such a nice house to come home to, and to ground herself. There was no place she enjoyed being as much as her own home. She'd bought it three years earlier; the year after her mother died. The house in which she and Ken had been raised was on Pennell Street, four blocks down Shore Road, and three blocks in, and while it was larger—it had four bedrooms and a finished basement—it wasn't on the shore.

It wasn't far, certainly, but Mary never walked by it and never drove past it, not because she had any unhappy memories associated with it, but because she didn't want to think about Ken, who was then living in Upstate New York. He ran a company in Binghamton that made photo albums, and lived in what Mary called "a nice house" in Selman's Falls, a town on the shore of Cayuga Lake. They hadn't seen each other for seven months. And there were no pictures of him anywhere in Mary's house—ironic, she would think, given the kind of business he ran—but there were no pictures of anyone in her house. Except on the two walls around the piano, where there was a portrait of Brahms as an old man—she found his widow's peak and full mustache and beard particularly distinguished—and a portrait of Schumann as a young man—she always thought he was handsome. The other walls were filled with the paintings and prints of Indian and Chinese art that the family had in their former home. Ken, though he was asked, decided to take nothing with him when he moved.

That first afternoon Mary lay in her bed, dozing on and off between calling Leila, Lizzy, Julietta, and Mel to let them know she was home but didn't want to be disturbed, and, five hours later, calling Leila, Lizzy, Julietta, and Mel to let them know she was home and had absolutely no problem being disturbed. Mel was thrilled, telling her that she would be "the next big thing," and when she asked him, "Why do you say 'big thing'? Why don't you mention a name?," he said, "Because big things don't stay big for very long. Except in exceptional circumstances." Mary could never tell, and wasn't sure she wanted to know, whether Mel was a bitter little man who didn't want anyone to be happier than he could make himself, or simply a pragmatist. So she didn't ask why her circumstance couldn't be exceptional.

Tuesday she spent doing what she usually did; practicing for three hours, as she had another concert, at which she would play her "winning" program, in two and a half weeks, and listening to music on her stereo. Mary had spent almost as much on her stereo equipment as most people spend on their houses. Like Macbeth, she bore a charmed life. But neither that nor much else she did was done to impress anybody but herself. She didn't invite people over to show off and say "Look at what *I* have." In fact, she almost never invited people over. She simply wanted to make herself as comfortable as she could, and in that way, she believed, she was nothing like Ken, who lived to impress others.

That afternoon she listened to Prokofiev's Symphony No. 4 in C major, Op. 112, her favorite of Prokofiev's seven symphonies, in the revised and expanded version, which she preferred; Schoenberg's Suite for Septet, Op. 29, which was scored for three clarinets—she *loved* the clarinet—string trio, and piano; and Ravel's *Ma mere l'oye*, the complete ballet, not the suite. In the weeks leading up to a concert, or days, depending on how much time she had between performances, she would listen to works by the composers she was going to perform, to remind herself how much she loved them, but *never* listen to different interpretations of whatever she would be playing, as that would only confuse her and make her question her own interpretive decisions.

And that night she ended up going out for dinner with Leila, Lizzy, and Julietta. They tried a new steakhouse called Alison Zolli's, that had just opened on Shore Road. When Mary tried a new restaurant, she liked doing it with friends, not because she wanted to hear their opinions but because eating with others took her mind away from the food and was something she didn't enjoy nearly as much as eating by herself. Which made it difficult for her to feel much enthusiasm for any untried eatery, but that let her feel more comfortable with following her routine; visiting the Pànduàn Room, her local Chinese restaurant of choice, every other Thursday night, and Sefaradi's, her local Italian restaurant of choice, on the Thursdays in between.

EVERYTHING FROM A TO Z said the sign outside Alison Zolli's, alluding to the owner's name, but Julietta complained that "All they have is *s*teak, *s*pinach, and other *s*hit, all too heavily *s*alted, and all with an *S*, so they seem to be about twenty-five letters short."

In fact, Mary agreed completely with what Julietta said, but resented her for saying it, because then it was no longer a vague notion with which she could agree or disagree; stating it made it a fact. What Mary really and always resented was how closely Julietta reminded her of her mother, who, according to Mary, found too many things to complain about, and left Mary questioning her own happiness, thinking that maybe most things she encountered weren't nearly as wondrous as they'd first seemed.

Still, their time together was at least moderately pleasant, and never once did they discuss Mary's win.

Wednesday followed similarly, though Mary, of course, listened to different pieces of music, but still by the same composers, and ate dinner alone, and then Thursday came. Thursday was her favorite day of the week.

When she was in school she always thought of Friday as the real beginning of the weekend. To her the weekend started late in the afternoon, when class let out, but even the hours leading up to it felt weekend*ish*, which made Thursday the last day of the school week or, later, for her friends and father, the work week, so the appropriate time to celebrate.

About four o'clock that afternoon, Mary walked into the living room to play some Brahms, a composer she hadn't listened to or played lately. She loved his late piano music; terse, concentrated, small pieces that were full of emotion, mostly melancholy and nostalgia, as was usual with Brahms, though her favorite among those pieces, and the one she was going to play, was the Intermezzo in C Major, Op. 119, No. 3, a seemingly but not quite happy work, and his next-to-last piece for solo piano. When she played it once for Leila, Leila laughed and said it reminded her of the Beatles' song *Maxwell's Silver Hammer*. And when Mary listened to that song she smiled and thought yes, she could hear the connection.

But walking into the living room that afternoon she felt a presence; something she'd never felt before, though living alone, she thought, must have heightened her sensitivity to it. Still, no one had ever hidden anywhere in her house, so she looked around before even getting to the piano, and breathed out a sigh, because she saw nobody. Hesitantly she walked over to the bench, placed the score she was carrying on the music rack, and sat down. Then she knew someone was looking at her, and when she turned around her senses went dead, because sitting on her couch were three identical figures, frozen as statues. From their skin and hair they looked like three elderly White men. Each was tall, at least six and a half feet in height, dressed in a dark blue serge suit, white cotton shirt, and light gray silk necktie, and each sat stock still with his palms turned down on his thighs. The creases in one figure's pants matched the creases in the pants of the other figures exactly, their navy socks fit snugly against their calves, and each wore a pair of black wingtips that were flawlessly polished. Only they had no faces. Which is to say, where their faces should have been were deep black chasms in which Mary could see snow falling, as though she were staring into a snow globe, but the snow was landing on nothing and was occasionally buffeted by what seemed like strong winds.

Then she broke into clear, pealing laughter. "Bravo!" she yelled. Of course the figures didn't move, because they couldn't. They were mannequins. What took her so long to realize that? Lizzy must have brought them there to scare her. And it didn't even occur to Mary to ask how Lizzy could have found or created figures that were so real, and then deliver them to Mary's house without her knowing it. Because Mary hadn't left her house since seeing Lizzy two nights earlier.

Why did she think Lizzy would have done that, rather than Leila or Julietta? Ashamed, she realized it was because Lizzy was White, and the skin of the mannequins, whose ears, necks, and hands she could see, was also white. Surely Leila or Julietta would have brought over figures whose skin was closer to the color of hers and theirs. But maybe, she thought, she was criticizing Lizzy for being different.

She continued to stare at the figures, wondering what mechanism was used to generate the illusion of falling snow, and her fascination, at least until then, outweighed her fear.

Then the first figure, the one who sat the farthest to Mary's left, raised his right hand, and Mary's vision went black, like a blink that lasted too long. When she was able to see again, she heard the first figure say, "We're quite real, Mary," as though he'd been reading her mind.

"But I didn't—," she said.

"See us?" he asked. "Of course not. "You won't see us from behind," the first figure said. "Only face-to-face."

At which the third figure laughed, because they had no faces.

Mary felt paper-thin, the way she would feel when she ran a high fever. "What am I looking at? Who are you? And who let you in?"

"We are the judges," the first judge said. "And we're here to judge you. As for who let us in, you did."

She might have just stepped into the elevator on the lowest floor of a building and felt it drop.

The third judge said brightly, "We could have worn masks, but we didn't want to scare you."

And Mary forced a laugh. "No. Bodies without faces are much less frightening."

"You know what we mean," the second judge said, shaking his head and placing his hands comfortably on either side of him, to show he was sympathetic. "You might have thought we were here to rob you."

Mary swallowed loudly. "Are you? And what do I need judges for?" she asked.

"To win," the first judge said, leaning forward. "You can't win unless you're judged."

Then the second judge quickly waved his hands in front of him. "But don't misunderstand us. We're not here to ensure you win any more competitions. You're not Faust and we aren't the Devil."

The first judge said, "As we explained already, we're here to judge you."

"On what?" Mary asked.

The three judges looked at each other, then the first judge said, "On everything."

"Why?" She sounded panicked, and the panic in her voice scared her almost as much as looking at the judges did.

"Because you like to be judged," the third judge said, looking as though he were about to stand for a moment. He cleared his throat.

At which Mary asked, "How can you speak if you have no mouths?"

"We have mouths," the second judge said. "You just don't see them."

"And we have eyes, too," said the third judge, "and we see everything you do."

"And hear everything, too. That's important," said the second judge.

Then Mary realized that they all spoke with the same voice. Clear of diction, slightly high-pitched, and what many people would call cultured, even aristocratic. "You all sound the same," she said.

"We speak with one voice," the first judge said. "That's essential for judging. We can't have division among us."

"Do you always agree?" she asked.

All three judges shrugged. Then the first judge nodded, the second judge shook his head, and the third judged moved his head diagonally.

They all laughed.

For a moment Mary berated herself for leading such an insular life, something she would think about often. A knock on the door or a telephone call would have been nice. But it was only her conversing with the judges. She didn't move from the piano bench. Looking confused, she asked, "What happens if I call the police?"

"You won't call the police, Mary," the second judge said, leaning forward and clasping his hands. She couldn't tell whether his tone was conciliatory or threatening, and then wondered why they kept repeating her name. Was it to remind themselves who they were talking to? Did they need to keep being reminded?

"Be*cause*," the first judge said, raising the index finger of his right hand, "they wouldn't see us."

"Or hear us," the second judge said.

"Only you can do that," the first judge said.

"But," the second judge said, "only when you're facing us. Try walking over to the recliner in the corner and tell us what you see."

So Mary walked over to the recliner and looked at the couch, but the judges were gone. Or at least seemed to be. "I can't see you," she said. "Are you there?" And then she yelled it. "Are you there?!" But there was only silence.

And yet, when she walked back to the piano and sat on the bench, the judges were sitting right in front of her, as she knew they would be.

"See?" the second judge said.

"One of the nice things about having three judges in your living room," the third judge said, "is that we don't take up space. So you can go about your daily routine and never know we're here. Because you won't see us and you won't hear us, unless you do exactly what you're doing now, which is sitting on the piano bench and looking at us."

"And in answer to your next question," the second judge said, and leaned back, which made Mary think his answer was going to be long, "no, it has nothing to do with your piano at all. You just have to be facing us to see and hear us."

"And no, we can't get off the couch," the third judge said. "But if you have guests, they can sit here very comfortably, and no one but you will be any the wiser. As long as you're in front of us. At which time you would basically see your guests superimposed on us."

The first judge looked behind him then turned to face Mary, who was shaking her head slowly. "So to return to your earlier questions," he said. "Why are we here? To judge you. And who invited us? You did."

"When?" Mary asked.

"When you won your competition and decided that you liked being judged."

"I never said that."

"You agreed with the judge's decision," the second judge said. "Which ultimately meant that you liked it, or you wouldn't have agreed with it. Winning and being judged can't be separated. They follow one another."

"When you're lucky," the third judge said under his breath.

"Am I lucky?" Mary asked.

"To win, yes," the first judge said. "But now? We're here neither to help you nor to hurt you. Only to judge you."

The third judge cleared his throat. "And I quote, 'What do you make of the judges' decision?' you were asked. And you said, 'What am I supposed to make of it? I'm glad they made it. I appreciate it.' I believe that's what was quoted in your interview."

INTERVIEWER: What do you make of the judges' decision?

MARY: What am I supposed to make of it? (*Laughs*) I'm glad they made it. I appreciate it.

INTERVIEWER: Do you think they made the right decision? Which is to ask, do you think you deserved to win?

MARY: What kind of question is that?

INTERVIEWER: The kind that warrants an answer? I ask because, let's be honest, performers don't always do their best, or think they've done their best, when they perform, even though their audience might think so.

MARY: I think I did well.

INTERVIEWER: Okay.

MARY: But you have to understand something. Competitions are easy.

INTERVIEWER: In what way?

MARY: I'm enormously critical of myself. I always have been. I'm not impossible to please, but close. So my own work doesn't always, or maybe doesn't often, satisfy me.

INTERVIEWER: I see.

MARY: But in a competition, I don't have to worry about that. I don't have to play better than I've ever played before, I only have to play better than everyone else is playing that night. And when you compare the number of times I've played something to the number of competitors I have, the odds are in my favor.

INTERVIEWER: I see. Okay. What was your motivation for winning? Why did you want to win?

MARY: To please myself.

INTERVIEWER: Did you want to win for the money?

MARY: Did you not just hear me? I said I wanted to win to please myself. I didn't need the money.

INTERVIEWER: The fame? The recording contract?

MARY: Are you hearing voices in your head? Because if you are, they're not mine. I played for myself and I always play for myself. To make myself proud. Because, ultimately, that's all that matters.

INTERVIEWER: We'll get back to that.

And Mary's face fell. "Are you working with the man who interviewed me?" she asked.

The first judge shook his head. "Not at all. In fact, we have no idea who he is."

"Or was," the second judge said.

"Nobody does," said the third judge quietly.

"I never saw it," Mary said, disappointed by the man's broken promise. "He never published the interview."

The first judge said, "It landed in the right hands."

Mary leaned back and depressed some of the piano keys with her left elbow, which startled her. "Then who sent you here? Did he?"

The first judge shook his head. Mary was wondering how much patience they would have for her, though they didn't seem to be answering her questions very directly, either.

The second judge sighed. "It couldn't have been him because we just told you that we don't know him."

"Do you believe in a higher power, Mary?" the first judge asked.

"I do," Mary said quickly, and nodded. She wasn't sure if she did, but figured that was what they wanted to hear.

"Then we were assigned to you. Does that make sense? Because people who believe in a higher power believe that every decision comes down from somewhere else. Either that or, because they believe that every decision comes down from somewhere else, or is made by somebody else, they end up believing in a higher power."

"And our credentials are impeccable," the third judge said. He cleared his throat. "We studied under Judge Asa Wyce. That's A-S-A W-Y-C-E."

What Mary then heard was, "That's A as in I, S as in C, A as in R, W as in Y, Y as in U, C as in Q, and E as in I," but what the third judge actually said, as he later explained, was, "That's 'A' as in 'aye,' 'S' as in 'see,' 'A' as in 'are,' 'W' as in 'why,' 'Y' as in 'you,' 'C' as in 'cue,' and 'E' as in 'eye.'" Proof, if any were needed, that most people don't pick up on the subtleties of the law.

The three judges laughed.

Mary, not knowing what to say or even what to think—how could she?—got up and stood in front of the first judge. "What's in there?" she asked, pointing to the chasm that would have been his face.

"Put your hand in and find out," he said. He shook his head. "It won't hurt. I promise."

Slowly she placed her left hand in, then her right hand, and when both hands were inside she felt what seemed like wind, but warm and damp, as if she'd just placed her wet hands beneath an electric dryer.

"You feel that?" the first judge asked.

"Yes," Mary said quietly.

"Those are ideas bouncing around. Or, rather, rushing. Because there's force behind them, isn't there?"

"There is," the third judge said.

Mary removed her hands and looked at them, noticing that nothing about their appearance had changed. Then the first judge said, "Okay, now try it again. Please. And you'll notice a difference."

And when she placed her hands inside a second time, a little more quickly and confidently than she had before, she felt nothing, but could still see the snow falling. Only the nothingness felt more profound, even excessive. Like the unworldly silence she'd experienced as a teenager when she took a hot air balloon ride.

"You don't feel anything now because you're being bombarded with ideas. But they have no substance. They're just, as you would say, abstract concepts."

"When did I say 'abstract concepts'"? Mary asked.

"In your interview," the first judge said.

"Of course," Mary said. "I remember that."

INTERVIEWER: Somebody once said that Beethoven's Ninth is a greater work than any performance could ever make it. What do you think of that?

MARY: I think that's nonsense. In the first place, I don't think Beethoven's Ninth is such a great work. He wrote much better pieces: the C-Sharp–Minor String Quartet, the *Hammerklavier Sonata*, the *Missa Solemnis*. But to get back to what you were saying, it's nonsense. Because a piece of music doesn't exist without a performance. It's not like a painting or a book that can just be seen and reveal itself. It needs to be *heard* and somebody has to make it heard. Otherwise it's only an abstract concept. Music is the art that walks on crutches; it can't stand by itself.

Mary finally realized that she felt dizzy, but attributed it to hunger because that was easier and more familiar than attributing it to fear. "I usually go out to eat on Thursday nights," she said.

"We know," said the second judge, shaking his head. "Don't let us stop you."

"And one more thing we should tell you, Mary," the first judge said.

"Yes?"

"You noticed how the snow appeared to fall exactly the same way when we were thinking about real ideas and when we were thinking about abstract concepts?"

She hadn't thought about it, but she nodded anyway.

"Well, the pattern of the snowfall never changes. It's no indication of what we're thinking. It's not like a facial expression, so you can't tell what's going on in our minds by looking at us."

"Justice shouldn't be wearing a blindfold," the third judge said, "she should be wearing a mask, because justice is inscrutable."

Ready to leave, though she was, Mary was so fascinated by the bizarrerie of the whole situation that she didn't want to walk away. Or so she told herself. But what was actually keeping her there was the fear that if she left, the three judges would ransack her house or plot something against her, or transform themselves into something more terrible when she got back. She never thought they'd be gone.

Noticing that she wasn't getting up, the first judge looked around and said, "Nice house you have here, Mary. Your parents must have left you well-off."

"You know they did," Mary said.

The first judge nodded. "We do. We just wanted to hear what you would say, because...you know. Sometimes, when people are being judged, they aren't always honest."

The second judge shook his head. "We don't," he said. "We know only what's presented to us, and your past hasn't been. Nor does it need to be. We won't and can't judge you on that."

"Wait a minute," Mary said. "I thought you all had to agree."

And the three of them laughed. For a moment Mary thought that one of their laughs was higher in pitch than the others but then realized that it seemed to float among them.

"All in fun," the third judge said. "The fact of the matter is, we didn't know. What you present to us is all that matters and all you can be judged on."

"We don't like the yellow walls," the first judge said, looking up.

"They aren't yellow; they're pale gold," Mary said.

"Yellow is the hue everything takes on when you develop cataracts," the first judge said. "It's the color of jaundiced skin."

"It's the color of *my* skin," Mary said, "and there's nothing wrong with that." Though she'd never made the connection, and doubted that was why she had the walls painted that way.

The second judge crossed his arms then let them fall into his lap. Nodding, he said, "Then if it doesn't bother you, it can't, of necessity, bother us." He might have added, "Do you understand who we are yet?" But Mary wouldn't have.

"Do you mind if I get up," she said, "and move to the recliner, where I won't see you?"

"Not at all," the first judge said, "but remember that we can still see you."

Although Mary was half Indian, nobody would have guessed it by looking at her. She had what Ken called, derisively, "the Chinese genes." She was short—five feet, four inches—but her legs were long and her torso compact so that, even at thirty, she looked like she'd just entered adolescence. Her skin was pale gold and smooth, her forehead tall, eyes wide-set, and nose small and upturned. She had her father's wide mouth but she smiled much less frequently than he did, yet when she did smile, it transformed her entire appearance. She wore her flat black hair at not quite shoulder length, parted on the right and combed behind her left ear but covering her right ear, the ear that her audiences would see when she performed, and that sometimes gave the impression that she was shutting them out.

When she started high school she befriended a boy named Ben Larsen who had what her father called a rubbery face. By which he meant it looked like it could be molded into different expressions without assuming its own expression naturally. The first time he met her, Ben said to Mary, "Don't take this the wrong way, but you Asians look so androgynous to me." Which Mary took as a sort of compliment, and she got into the habit, for a while, of being photographed from her chin up so nobody could see that she didn't have an Adam's apple. But then she decided that Ben couldn't respect who she was or appreciate her difference, and they stopped speaking to each other before the end of that semester. Ben died of a ruptured appendix a year later, but Mary would never be sure how she felt about that. Sitting on the recliner that night, she decided to think about him rather than the judges, as she had no idea what they were thinking about. So she got up and walked back to the piano bench because she didn't like being looked at by people she couldn't see.

"Again, nice house, Mary," the first judge said. "But carpeting? How old-fashioned. No hardwood floors?"

Mary didn't like hardwood floors. "I'll have hardwood floors when they bury me," she said. "That'll be enough."

Clearly, she thought, it was time to leave. Confused and terrified, but also intrigued and excited, she stepped out, knowing that things would look very different when she got home.

She decided to walk rather than drive to the Pànduàn Room. As I explained, Mary didn't like being outside, and would walk only when she felt her mood needed improving, as she certainly did that night. But walking improved her mood in a particular way. It made her happy when she stopped and was back inside, among the things she found comforting and familiar. That said, she rarely drove to the restaurant that time of year, because it didn't have its own parking lot, there was little on-street parking available, and the nearest municipal lot was several blocks away.

The Pànduàn Room was located on Lampert Street, half a block to the right of Shore Road, when heading south, so away from the shore. It was small, as restaurants go, especially in a town with a large influx of tourists, but the tourists came primarily during the summer, and the restaurant was open all year long. Outside there was a patio with terra cotta tiles, holding six tables with umbrellas and beach chairs, and inside there was a small entryway, curtained with strings of colored glass beads, and four separate rooms holding three tables each. Each room was painted a different color—dark green, dark red, dark brown, or dark orange—though there were enough windows with open shudders to prevent it from looking gloomy. Mary found the atmosphere caressing.

It was the only Chinese restaurant she knew, which is to say, the only Chinese restaurant she'd ever been to, that wasn't staffed entirely by Chinese people, as all the servers were White. She never understood why Chinese restaurants, more than other ethnic eateries, tended to be so ethnically homogeneous. She'd been to many Italian restaurants where the wait staff wasn't Italian, Mexican restaurants where the wait staff wasn't Mexican, and Jewish delicatessens where the wait staff wasn't Jewish, or at least didn't look as though they were.

She then thought about what it meant to "look Jewish," and decided that the descriptor made no sense. It was easy enough to tell if a person was Asian or Black or Hispanic, but Judaism was a religion and religions were founded on shared beliefs. It could be argued that Jews descended from a particular geographic place, the Middle East, which would attribute certain physical characteristics to them, but Judaism was a minority religion; most people from the Middle East weren't Jewish. So to say somebody "looked Jewish," she decided, was as silly as saying that somebody "looked like blue was his favorite color."

The hostess—Elsie, she'd said her name was, or was it LC?—showed Mary to a table in the dark orange room, which was otherwise unoccupied, and handed her a menu. Then Jesse, her usual and favorite waiter, walked over, placing a glass of ice water, a pot of tea, a teacup in a saucer, a small wooden bowl of crispy noodles, two porcelain bowls of pale yellow mustard and duck sauce, and a white linen napkin inside of which was wrapped the silverware—a fork, soup spoon, and teaspoon; because this was an old-fashioned Chinese restaurant, there was no knife—in front of her.

"So how are you doing tonight?" Jesse asked, carefully pouring tea into her cup. He held a napkin around the handle of the teapot, both so he wouldn't burn himself and to let her know it was hot.

Jesse was in his early twenties and had a round face, dark brown hair that perpetually looked like he'd gotten a crew cut the month before, dark brown eyes that squinted slightly, a sharp nose, and a relaxed smile. His body was on the cusp between muscular and corpulent, so that while he wasn't at all fat, you could imagine him turning heavy or, just as easily, sculpted, and that leap of the imagination helped many people see him as handsome.

"How am I doing?" Mary asked. "Do you have half a lifetime? Pull up a chair and I'll tell you."

Jesse grinned. He would never laugh because he thought laughing at a customer was rude. "I'll give you a few moments to look over the menu, then I'll come back," he said.

But Mary didn't want him to go, so she shook her head and tightened the expression on her face. "I'm doing well, thank you," she said. "And you?"

Jesse put on a more natural smile. "Glad to hear it," he said. "I'm fine."

And Mary wished he hadn't said that: "Glad to hear it." Not because it sounded insincere; Jesse never sounded insincere, but because her mother had used that expression all her life. "Good morning, child," she would say every day when Mary woke up and came into the kitchen to prepare breakfast. "How are you today?" And Mary would say "Good," or "Okay," or, later, "Well," and her mother would say, "Glad to hear it," in the same benignly uninflected voice, over and over, day after day, year after year, to the point where it became nearly crippling, because Mary thought that if she weren't doing well, if something really were wrong, she couldn't let her mother know because that would disappoint her and leave Mary feeling guilty. Which may have been one reason why Mary grew up hating what she saw as the need or desire to please others; a trait she thought her brother carried to excess.

And then, in the wake of her win at the Graffman competition, she especially didn't want to be reminded of her mother, who wasn't with her anymore.

"Daddy," she'd said to her father when she was seven, "do people still live after they die?"

And he'd said, "Are you asking me if there's life after death?"

And she'd said she guessed so.

And her father had said, "Absolutely, yes. I believe there is. Of course you might not, sweetheart; you'll have to decide that for yourself"—as far as Mary was concerned, her father never treated her like a child—"but I think they do."

"But what if you're wrong?" she'd asked.

And her father had laughed and said, "Then that will save me the need of kicking myself for being such a fool once I'm gone."

Mary looked over the menu, but more to impress Jesse than because she needed to find anything. She always knew what she was going to order before she got there, and the menu, for as long as she'd been visiting, never changed. But she thought that if she simply closed it and laid it aside, she would be doing a disservice to whoever took the time to put it together in the first place. Which likely wouldn't have been Jesse, but he did work there.

A few minutes later, walking back to Mary's table, Jesse asked, "So what'll it be tonight?"

Mary lifted her eyes to him. "You mean you haven't figured me out yet?"

A quick smile. "In what way?"

"There are five dishes I order, cyclically, whenever I come here." She switched to a look of disappointment. "Or hadn't you noticed? Shrimp with walnuts, chow som shee, char siu, chajangmyun, and hot pot. Anyway, tonight it's going to be the char siu. With, of course, the usual bowl of Chinese watercress soup to start."

A more effusive smile. "You're being serious, aren't you?"

She laughed. "Yes, for better and worse, I live on structure." She leaned back, noticing how tense she was.

"So you wouldn't be interested in trying something new," Jesse said.

"What's new?" Mary asked. "And please don't say 'New York and New Jersey.'"

Jesse shook his head. "Never heard that one. No, tonight we're offering Thai hot wings. Something different. And if the guests like it, we may add it to our menu, Dennis says." Dennis Gee was the owner and general manager. Then Jesse seemed to relax. "They're chicken wings glazed with peanut, basil, garlic, and lime sauce, and served with ginger and scallion chutney on the side. They're eight ninety-five for six or thirteen ninety-five for a dozen."

She smiled. "Thank you for telling me how much they cost," she said. "I hate it when I walk into a restaurant and the server reads me a list of specials and doesn't include the price. I refuse to order anything unless I know how much I'm paying for it."

"So would you like them?" Jesse asked, and Mary was surprised at how disinterested he sounded in what she thought was a compliment.

"I'll take the six, please."

"Six? You got it. And the soup, too?"

"Yes, please. The soup, too."

"Oh, and on the subject of branching out," Jesse said, "where did you park?"

"I didn't park anywhere," Mary said. "I walked here. Why?" She was afraid she sounded scornful.

"Because, as you know, we don't have a parking lot, but Phoebe's, the coffee shop next door—"

"How ironic to have a coffee shop next to a Chinese restaurant."

Jesse, unexpectedly, laughed, and then, controlling himself, said, "Yes. So Phoebe's, next door, has opened their parking lot to our customers."

Which was either very nice, Mary thought, or a way to make Phoebe's parking lot more crowded and, thus, make that establishment look more desirable, because Phoebe's was never busy, though Mary loved going there. "Thank you," she said. "I'll remember that next time."

A few minutes later Jesse brought over the soup. She stared at him, thinking about how young he was and how impressive he looked in his starched white shirt and narrow black bowtie and black slacks, like a child trying to look grown up, though she knew she didn't find him attractive.

"I figured I'd space the soup and the wings," he said. "Unless you'd like them together."

"No," she said. "Spacing is fine."

It would certainly extend the length of her meal, and she was glad to be away from home, unusual for her, because, just then, the judges were occupying it. Naturally she thought of them, but was surprised to realize she could have put them out of her mind for as long as she already had.

She wasn't used to feeling threatened, never really having been threatened by anything or anyone before—no "Wait 'til your father gets home" or any other such nonsense while she was growing up—and she wasn't sure that the judges were or could be threatening. But then her stomach dropped as she thought about being judged and what might happen if they, for lack of a better term, ruled against her. But she didn't know what she was going to be judged on, what criteria they could possibly use, or what the consequences or rewards—funny how she wasn't thinking about rewards—would be. But all that, she assumed, would be explained to her later. Unless things worked out the way they did when others judged her, and she could simply ignore what they said, though, since that evolved over a lifetime, it always took a lifetime to attain.

Jesse brought over the wings, setting the plate carefully down in front of her and removing her soup bowl, then setting down a smaller dish filled with the chutney.

She felt obligated to at least taste one wing while he was standing there and let him know that she liked it—she would tell him that even if she didn't—but then realized that Jesse made a mistake and brought her a dozen wings instead of six. Dipping her first wing into the chutney and taking a bite of it, she then yelled, "Jesse! You made a mistake. You brought me twelve wings instead of six."

Jesse smiled and said, "No mistake. My treat."

Well, hmm, Mary thought. What was she supposed to say? Why did he do it? The first thing that crossed her mind was that he was being flirtatious. He had, after all, made her a present of, yes, six chicken wings, and Mary was sure that other people had been won over by less. But she always thought that way; Mary, who'd never been on a date because she never had the sexual or emotional desire to do so. The second thought that crossed her mind was...well, there was no second thought. Jesse wasn't trying to screw Dennis by serving a larger portion for the price of a smaller one. She was sure he respected Dennis too much. And the difference would have come out of his own pocket. He had, after all, said "My treat," not "Compliments of the house." So maybe he was just being nice and had no reason other than that, but that disappointed her, and she felt sad that she couldn't appreciate it when somebody did something nice for her and didn't expect anything in return. Fortunately, the wings were delicious and she knew she would order them again. The next time they were on the menu.

A moment later Jesse came back with a plate holding a large, wet, steaming hand towel. "I'm not implying anything," he said, suppressing a smile. "But if you find things getting sticky—"

"Jesse," she said, and nodded, "thank you very much." She liked repeating his name. She knew the towel would be cold and barely damp by the time she used it, but that was okay.

A few minutes after that, Jesse returned with a sizzling platter holding the char siu in one hand, and a steak knife in the other. He smiled as he put them down because he saw the plate of twelve clean bones sitting in front of Mary. "Enjoy?" he asked.

"They were delicious," Mary said.

"I'm glad. So how's Ken?" Jesse asked. "May I venture?"

Mary thought Jesse found Ken sexually attractive. She could tell by the way Jesse had looked at him seven months earlier, the last time Ken came to visit, and they'd eaten at the Pànduàn Room, and Jesse seemed very impressed that Ken owned a company that made photo albums. Jesse hadn't realized that people still collected photographs. Ken told him he'd be surprised. Mary thought back to her first photo album, which her father had bought her when she was six. It was a nice leather-covered binder holding black sheets of what her father called "Something one grade up from construction paper," on which she would stick four small plastic red tabs into which she would insert each picture. Ken's products were nice, she told Jesse, but Ken, she said, had no sense of remembrance and found his choice of a job very ironic. Mary would constantly bring up the fact that Ken had a girlfriend, to let Jesse down gently, if that's what she was doing, but she liked thinking that Jesse was gay so she wouldn't become offended by the thought that he might be coming on to her.

"Can you sit down?" Mary asked.

Jesse shook his head. "Dennis wouldn't approve."

"Dennis isn't here," Mary said. "Or am I missing something?"

"He has people who watch."

Mary moved her napkin around her lap, then stared at it. "Dennis with the painted smile."

Jesse looked taken aback. "I think it's real. He's just happy. He has plenty to be happy about."

Mary turned to him. "*You* think. That doesn't matter." She smiled derisively. "There are plenty of people who we think should be happy, but aren't." She took a sip of water. "They have their reasons. Like Ken, about whom you were just asking." Mary dipped a single crispy noodle in the duck sauce, placed it in her mouth, chewed it, swallowed it, then rolled her eyes. "So you want to know how he is?" She shrugged her shoulders and shook her head. "Same as ever." Her smile turned wry. "I will say this for him. He's my one constant in a world that's always changing. Don't get me wrong, I haven't spoken to him in months. But why do I need to? It's always the same thing. He calls, he asks me for money, I tell him no. He calls, he asks me for money, I tell him no. He calls, he asks me for money, I tell him no. Do you see where this is going? And I don't know why. He *has* a good job. Or *had* one the last time we spoke. And his girlfriend, the current one...," she cupped her hands around her mouth, "*Now serving number...,*" then rested them in her lap, "is well-off. But that's what's going on with him. I just don't know where his money goes."

Jesse looked abashed. "You know what's funny?" he asked. "Or sad?" And his expression hinted more at sadness than it did mirth. "In millions of homes, bars, and restaurants across America right now, this exact same conversation is being repeated. Only the names have been changed to protect the innocent."

Mary couldn't believe Jesse would know that expression from a television show that was popular when her father was growing up. "How old are you?" she asked.

"Twenty-two," he said.

And yeah, she thought; kids today know everything. But part of knowing everything meant being able to see past what was close and familiar, a habit Mary never had, either because of the way she was raised or, more likely, natural inclination. Yet she admired it in others, so, picking up on what Jesse had said, she asked, "So tell me. How's the wife and kids?"

For a moment Jesse didn't know what she was talking about but then suddenly laughed, showing his long white teeth that Mary thought made him look almost handsome, and said, "Doing good. But, you know, the kids'll be going off to college soon, so we've got to start saving for that."

And Mary shook her head sadly, thinking about how many people were having *that* conversation, and wondered how and why straightjacketing people into conventional lives was supposed to be attractive. You get married, you have kids, you raise a family. None of it held the slightest interest for her. "I love you, I must see you again, but fetters I will not wear." Brahms had said that to a woman friend of his. He never married and never settled down with anyone. But Mary knew that most people, or so it seemed, didn't think that way, and she didn't know how Jesse thought. So leaning back and feigning tiredness, she asked for the check.

"Sure. Just a second," he said. "How much older is Ken than you?"

"Four years," Mary said. "You know, it takes us four years to replace a president. Usually. But Ken? He always stays on."

Jesse brought Mary the check, which was enclosed in a small leather folder. "Thank you as always," he said, sounding perhaps a bit formal. But then he relaxed again and said, "You eat here every other week, don't you?"

Mary nodded. "That's right. And on the alternate weeks, usually Thursdays, I eat Italian."

She didn't want to explain herself to Jesse, especially as what she said sounded, to her, like an excuse, but she was sure he was going to ask her why she didn't eat at the Pànduàn Room every week, so she explained herself anyway. She hated being pushed into a corner by questions she otherwise didn't want to answer, but as long as it was her decision, she didn't mind talking about anything.

"Which one do you go to?" Jesse asked.

"Sefaradi's," Mary said.

"Never been."

"Really?! How long have you lived here?"

"I don't live here," Jesse said. "I live in East Glouby and just drive here to work every day."

"That far?"

Jesse shrugged. "I like it. I used to work as far south as Menhaden Bay."

"They have restaurants there?!"

"Yes," Jesse said, raising his eyebrows. "And people eat there, too."

Mary shook her head and laughed to cover her embarrassment. "You know what I mean. So before I found Sefaradi's, I used to eat at Guido di Zio's, because that's where my parents took us. They loved it, but what do an Indian man and a Chinese woman know about good Italian food?"

"This sounds like the beginning of a bad joke," Jesse said.

What does a Chinese woman know about good Italian food? Why did you ask that, Mary? What were *you*? It's one thing to pull away from other people, but you should never pull away from yourself.

Mary sighed. "It was really nice, and very friendly, but the food just wasn't that good."

Jesse nodded. "There are a lot of places like that. It makes you wonder why people go to certain restaurants, or restaurants in general. In some cases I'm sure it's not for the food."

INTERVIEWER: Do you go to a lot of live performances? You must.

MARY: Must I? I don't.

INTERVIEWER: Why not?

MARY: Why not? Because they have little to do with music. They're social events, not musical ones. At least not primarily. If I want to listen to something, I mean *really* listen to it, I'll put on a recording. That way it's just me and the music. No other people around, which I find distracting. I even find it distracting having to look at a performer, so on the rare occasion I do go to a concert, I sit through it with my eyes closed. Just as I do when I listen to music at home. And if I'm in the mood for a particular piece, I can hear it at my leisure. When I want to. When I go to a concert I know what's going to be played, but I don't know if I'm going to be in the mood for it at the time it's performed.

"Do you ever eat Indian out?" Jesse asked. He knew Mary's background and had met Ken, who looked noticeably Indian.

"I don't," Mary said. "Nobody cooked better Indian food than my mother, so I don't bother. I try, and can do pretty well at home, but I can't cook like her."

"So what do you do for Indian food, then?"

"Remember how good it was."

Then she had to decide how much of a tip to leave, and that actually troubled her. The bill came to forty-two dollars and sixty-seven cents. She routinely left a fifty percent tip, which would have meant twenty-one dollars, and she knew Jesse was used to it. Julietta had once criticized her for leaving such large tips. "You're only trying to show off how rich you are," she'd said. She didn't always understand Mary. In fact, Mary left large tips because her first roommate at NYU was a psychology major named Ossie Magoulnik, who spent part of her time working as a waitress at a nearby Irish pub called Maggie Yarnes'. And after stopping in to say hello and be served by her one night, Mary realized how harried and frazzled Ossie was, so she decided to leave her a large, fifty percent, tip. The next morning Ossie told Mary that she didn't have to do that, but Mary could see how much Ossie appreciated it.

But Jesse had paid, or would be paying, five dollars, presumably from his own pocket, for the additional chicken wings he gave her. So Mary left a twenty-six dollar tip for Jesse; the twenty-one dollars she'd originally planned on, plus the five dollars to cover the cost of the extra wings. For a moment she wondered if that would be insulting; basically telling Jesse that she didn't want any part of her meal to be paid for. But she left the money anyway, and thought that maybe she was just being nice for the sake of being nice, and in that way she was able to appreciate what Jesse had done.

She enjoyed her walk home but felt her throat tighten as she got to her house, because she could tell from the outside that somebody had shut off the living room light. It had to have been one of the judges, but Mary then remembered, or thought she remembered, their telling her that they couldn't get off the couch. Which made Mary think there could be other beings in her house, the house that was, until earlier that afternoon, occupied only by her.

The brass lamp next to the recliner was always lit, night and day, to provide enough light for the whole house when, say, Mary got up in the middle of the night and walked into the kitchen for a snack. She didn't bother shutting it off during the day because, frankly, she hated variety. So then she wished she hadn't gone out, so she could have seen what happened—she was right; she couldn't trust them—but if her house was no longer going to be hers alone, she didn't want to stay in it all the time.

Then, opening the front door, there was another surprise. She saw a large projection screen standing in front of the lamp and the recliner. Home movies?, she thought, but couldn't laugh. Too much had changed since she'd won the competition, and she wondered if none of it would have happened if she'd lost. Was it worth it? She didn't know yet; it was too early to tell.

"What's going on here?" she asked.

But, of course, her question was met with silence because she could neither hear nor see the judges until she stood in front of them.

So walking to the piano bench and facing them she repeated her question. Then she heard a whistle, which shook her, and the first judge said, "Mary, take a seat. We've come to a decision."

For a moment she thought he was going to tell her that they'd decided to leave, but she knew that wasn't what he meant.

"We've made a ruling," the second judge said.

The third judge cleared his throat, but said nothing.

"Okay, first you have to understand how such rulings work," said the first judge.

"Where did you get the screen?" Mary asked. "It's not mine." And she began picking at the sleeves of her blouse as though trying to rid it of lint. Then, looking at the cocktail table, she noticed that somebody had set up an old carousel slide projector there, which wasn't hers, either.

"You'll see that we put felt cups underneath the feet of the projector, so as not to mark your table," the second judge said amiably.

"Where did you get the projector?" Mary asked, surprising herself by how exhausted she sounded.

"The projector and the screen are ours," the first judge said. "We come prepared. But don't worry, you won't see them once the show is over."

"Until it's time for the next show," the third judge said, and nodded.

"What show? What next show?!"

"Mary, I wish I could stand, but I can't," the first judge said. "Then I could pat you on the shoulder and calm you down."

Patting Mary on the shoulder was no way to calm her down.

"So please just sit on the piano bench and listen to what we have to say. This won't take long, and then you'll have the whole night to yourself."

"Remember, if you sit or stand anywhere else, you won't know we're here."

"But what about the screen and the projector? I'll still see them."

The first judge, sounding a little irritated, said, "You won't see them anymore when this is over."

And that scared Mary, but the second judge said, "Not to worry."

To lighten the mood, she said, "I can't believe you found a projector and screen that are so old. I haven't seen anything like them in years."

"Like you," the second judge said, emphasizing his words, "we like what's familiar."

And Mary thought back to the interviewer and his yellow legal pad, black ballpoint pen, and cassette recorder.

"So here's what's going to happen," the first judge said, leaning back. "We're going to show you slides of the incident on which we've passed judgment. We ask that you don't say anything or ask us any questions during our presentation, unless it's to answer a question we've put to you. There might and probably will be some of those. We will then tell you what our judgment is. Then the projector and screen will disappear and you can ask us anything you like."

"This is a dream, isn't it?" Mary said, trying to smile.

"If it is," the third judge said, "it's a dream you're not going to wake up from."

"Again," the first judge said, "We're here neither to help you nor to hurt you. We're here only to judge you."

The projector was turned on and Mary saw the outside of the Pànduàn Room. She was sure she remembered that picture from the restaurant's website, which she visited often to study their large menu, so Mary wasn't sure how the judges had a slide of it, but didn't think to ask them.

"This is the Pànduàn Room at number 6712 Lampert Street, Ardell, New Jersey. But you know that already," the first judge said. "Next slide please, Mr. Slide-Advancer."

And the third judge, who'd been holding in his left hand a remote control attached by a cord to the projector, pushed a small red button, and the slide advanced noisily.

"Exhibit A," the first judge said, and the third judge laughed. "You, Mary Sorabi, sitting at your table at the Pànduàn Room."

Mary's eyes bugged out as she saw a picture of her that must have been taken just an hour before. "How? Where did you get that?"

The first judge held up his right hand. "No questions, Mary. Next slide please, Mr. Slide-Advancer."

"Exhibit B," the first judge said. "Jesse Callister, your server."

And the next slide showed Jesse pouring the tea into her teacup, holding a napkin around the handle of the teapot.

Hmm, Mary thought. I never knew his last name. But why would I?

"Do you need to see more?" the first judge asked. "A rhetorical question; we'll show you, anyway."

And over the course of the next five minutes they showed her thirty-seven slides that must have been taken during the dinner she'd just eaten, but the judges swore that they simply "were given them" and "didn't take them." Which was to say, they hadn't been spying on her with a camera while she ate.

"So here was the situation on which we passed or, I should say, on which we *decided to pass*, judgment. You can turn the lights on," the first judge said, and as the brass lamp on the drum table illuminated, the projector and screen disappeared, as though someone had suddenly stopped thinking about them. "The question was, should you or should you not have paid Jesse the five dollars for the extra wings he brought you?"

Mary laughed. "That's what I'm being judged on?"

"It is," said the second judge. "But please look at it in its proper context. You had a judgment to make. And it was a situation to which you gave a fair amount of thought, didn't you? Surely you realize that you did, Mary."

She did. And she stopped laughing when she realized that it was decisions like that, small decisions, that basically carried her through life. At first she thought that only people like her mother, whom she did love and remembered affectionately, tied themselves up in, or tied themselves down with, such minutiae, but even big decisions were nothing but a lot of small decisions piled on top of one another. So maybe it was more fair for the judges to judge her on numerous small acts rather than on single large ones. She wondered if they were trying to teach her something about herself.

The second judge continued. "Then we had a judgment to make. It always works that way. If our judgment agrees with yours, we record it as a positive judgment, though I wouldn't read too much into the word 'positive.' If our judgment doesn't agree with yours, we record it as a 'negative' judgment."

"Though I wouldn't read too much into the word 'negative,' either," the third judge said, leaning forward and extending his right arm.

"But what makes one of us right and the other wrong?" Mary asked, leaning carefully back against the piano so she wouldn't depress the keys.

"An excellent question," the first judge said. "Rather than think of these judgments in terms of right and wrong, think of them in terms of agreement and disagreement. Accord and discord."

"Is agreement always better?" Mary asked, suddenly leaning forward.

The judges looked at each other, and the second judge said, "You tell us. We're just following your line of thinking."

"But to get back to what we were saying," the first judge said, "the question was whether you should or should not have given Jesse the extra five dollars. The argument *for*, please."

The second judge leaned forward. "The argument *for*," he said. "is simple, and there's much to be said for it. You didn't want the five dollars to come out of Jesse's pocket."

"That said," the third judge said, "you might also have been trying to show off, by leaving what most people would think of as a very excessive tip."

"How is that the argument *for*"? the second judge asked.

"It could help Mary feel good about herself," the third judge said, "by reminding her of what she has."

The second judge nodded and sat back.

"The argument *against*, please," the first judge said.

"As you yourself thought—," said the third judge

"You can read my mind," Mary said.

"We can't," the first judge said. "We just know how to pick up on cues."

"So the argument *against*," the third judge said, "is that you were basically handing back the gift Jesse gave you. Just transformed from six chicken wings into money, but still handing it back. Which could be seen as a form of rejection."

Mary shook her head. Was this *really* what got her through life?

"But ultimately," the first judge said, raising the index finger of his right hand, "we find in your favor. We agree with you. We're in accord."

Mary looked around her dumbly. "So what do I get as a result of that? What do I get for my 'win'?"

"The advantage," the first judge said, "is that everything in your life remains status quo. As it was."

"What kind of advantage is that?!" Mary asked.

"You're the last person who should be asking that, Mary," the second judge said. "Isn't status quo what you like?"

"From what we've observed, it is," the third judge said.

The first judge leaned back and sunk his shoulders deeply into the backrest. "And there's nothing wrong with that. Because yours is a good life. A great life, even. A rare life. Most people would love their lives disrupted or shaken up somehow, because they don't really appreciate them. They find them acceptable, so-so, but boring. Dull. You don't. You love the life you have. So stick with it."

"Learn to enjoy it more," the third judge said.

"I do enjoy it," Mary said.

And the first judge said, "Sometimes." He crossed his legs.

"Now it's time for questions," the second judge said.

"I don't have any questions," Mary said, shaking her head and straightening her skirt.

"But we do," said the third judge.

"Oh."

"Mary," the first judge said, uncrossing his legs. "Do you have any friends?"

"Yes," Mary said, swallowing. "Three very good friends. Leila, Lizzy, and Julietta. You must know that."

"Tell us about those friends, Mary," the first judge said.

And the third judge said, "We're your Holy Trinity now."

Mary didn't understand that and didn't like it, because she found nothing holy about her friends or about her feelings toward them. Then she decided that the third judge was making a joke. Much later she would wonder why the judges never asked if she had a boyfriend or a girlfriend or had ever been married or was dating somebody. The fact of the matter was, as I've already explained, she really didn't think much about people sexually, and realized one morning, when she woke up, that she had no sexual desire for anyone. She fell back asleep and slept profoundly well after that. Sometimes she told herself that, if anybody asked, she would say that her love for music took the place of, or absorbed, her love for other people, but that was too easy, too pat. Life isn't built on cause-and-effect relationships, and nobody's life follows a smooth narrative path. There are no straight lines in nature.

So after she described Leila, Lizzy, and Julietta to them, surprising herself with how comfortable she felt during the conversation, the first judge said, "Then Jesse is not your friend."

She shook her head. "I wouldn't think of him as one, no. In fact, I didn't even know his last name."

"Then that should be it for tonight. We'll see you the next time."

"Won't you always be here?" she asked, and thought her question sounded needier than she meant it to.

"You can always see us," the first judge said, "but sitting here like statues, if you face us. The way we appeared the first time you saw us. We won't move or talk unless we have something to say, which means unless we've reached a judgment. Until then, no, we're inaccessible. Good night, Mary."

And they assumed their frozen postures, their black wingtips flawlessly polished, their navy socks fitting snugly against their calves, and the creases in one judge's pants matching the creases in the pants of the other judges exactly.

Two days later, on Saturday, Mary did her grocery shopping. She'd seen, but hadn't heard from, the judges since. Of course she hadn't done much other than practice and listen to music, and she couldn't imagine being judged on that. And she hadn't spoken with or texted her friends, though that was not unusual.

Mary visited the local ShopRite, which was two miles down Shore Road, every other Saturday. She'd been going there since she was a child, when her mother would take her shopping every weekend, and she loved, as most children do, sitting in the child seat of the shopping cart and letting her legs dangle through the leg holes. When they approached an electric door, which held an unusual fascination for Mary, her mother would turn the cart around so that the door faced Mary, who could then see what it looked like to enter the store. Then her mother would turn the cart back and push it by the handle. Mary never forgot that.

That Saturday Mary was, unsurprisingly, thinking about the judges on her drive there. She would never mention them to, or discuss them with, anybody. No one, she was sure, would believe her, and some people, she was equally sure, would think she'd lost her mind. The three judges, she decided, had subtly different personalities, and though she'd spoken to them for less than twenty minutes in total, they'd made a deep impression on her. Of course. The first judge, she thought, was the most pragmatic, the second judge the most compassionate or sympathetic, and the third judge found humor where the other two didn't.

When she passed Coralis Avenue, she knew she was halfway there. It was the only road in Ardell as wide as Shore Road, and it conveniently separated the town, almost evenly, into a North Side and a South Side. The North Side was entirely residential while the South Side was commercial. The Pànduàn Room sat a few blocks north of Coralis Avenue, but the ShopRite was much farther south, almost at the end of town, which was the border with Port Elroy. Mary loved shopping there to a degree she found unusual, and looked forward so much to her biweekly outings that she sometimes counted down the days until she would be there again. She could, of course, go shopping any time she wanted, and would often run in for stray items, but on these alternate Saturdays she came with a big list and spent almost an hour in the store.

The reason she loved it so much was that it reminded her of her mother, and of her growing up with her mother. Not as it *really* happened, but as it happened in her memory. In reality, her mother could be difficult: negative, finding faults where Mary couldn't see them, depressed, and always complaining about how lonely she was. That in spite of the fact that she had a larger family and more friends than almost anybody Mary knew, and with whom her mother would spend much of her time. Still, little that Mary or Ken or even Vim did seemed to please her, and Mary sometimes wavered between simply giving up trying to make her happy and feeling that it was her fault that her mother wasn't happy. But in retrospect, all of that sadness and frustration disappeared, and Mary could selectively recall the love, warmth, compassion, and support that her mother had no real trouble showing, and Mary thought maybe it was because her mother was gone, so there was no reality to interfere or conflict with her more positive memories.

INTERVIEWER: Do you like chamber music?

MARY: I love chamber music. More than orchestral music. I guess because of the intimacy. And I listen to it more than any other kind of music, even piano music, but I just won't play it.

INTERVIEWER: What's your favorite piece of chamber music that involves the piano?

MARY: Brahms' First Violin Sonata. Without question.

INTERVIEWER: Why?

MARY (*Laughs*): For reasons that have absolutely nothing to do with music.

INTERVIEWER: Would you like to tell me what those reasons are?

MARY: Sure. I grew up in Ardell, but went to college in New York, at NYU. And my first year there I missed my friends terribly, because they were the kids I'd grown up with and gone to school with for so many years. Anyway, my first semester, I didn't come home to visit until Thanksgiving. So after celebrating with my family on Thursday, I spent all day Friday with my friends. And that night, after I got home, I listened, for maybe the second time, to Brahms' First Violin Sonata, because it was part of a recording I'd just bought, featuring all three of his violin sonatas.

INTERVIEWER: Okay.

MARY: Saturday I spent with my family again, and then on Sunday afternoon I drove back to school, and took the discs with me. But here's the thing. Every time I heard that piece, from that time on, all I could think about was them. Not really them, my friends, more the time we'd spent together. So while the music was playing, and I was listening to it, I was reliving the day we'd shared. But, now stop me if this sounds strange, it felt *better* than the time I'd spent with them.

INTERVIEWER: Why?

MARY: I really don't know. Maybe because I was alone, and I just enjoy being by myself more than I enjoy being with other people. But I was more relaxed, more comfortable, more happy. I wasn't worried that I was going to say something or do something that they didn't want to hear or didn't like, or they were going to say or do something I didn't want to hear or didn't like. I was just reliving the day without any of its attendant worries and anxieties.

INTERVIEWER: What happened the next time you saw them?

MARY: I saw them only twice more after that, but neither time was any fun. I couldn't recapture that magic. *By being with them*. If I wanted to recapture that magic, all I had to do was listen to the music, and there it was. But after that I didn't want to see them anymore.

INTERVIEWER: Because it wasn't as much fun as that weekend was.

MARY: Because it wasn't as much fun *as the way I remembered* that weekend being whenever I listened to the music.

The music had preserved that weekend in an idealized state. But memory is rarely accurate. As Mary once said to me, "Faulty memory is not a result of age; it's a result of desire."

Mary spent more than an hour in the supermarket that Saturday afternoon. She found herself walking more slowly than she usually would, to the consternation of some of the other shoppers, but a lot of people trudged through the aisles. She wanted to absorb as much memory of her mother as she could. Her mother who also, incidentally, tended to walk very slowly. Mary didn't give a lot of thought to it, but I think it was because of the judges. She was escaping, though "escaping" is too negative a word, her present, which was very uncertain, and running back to her past, which had already been established, so she knew how everything turned out.

The shortest checkout line she could find was line number 10, where there were only two people ahead of her: a balding, pudgy, tanned man in late middle age, who was wearing a dark brown t-shirt, khaki shorts, and boat shoes, and an older woman, likely in her seventies, with a surprisingly small face and unkempt white hair wrapped in a pear green headscarf, who wore an oversized lilac pullover, distended at the neck, and a light pink windbreaker—wasn't it too warm for that?—that Mary thought was more appropriate for a child of seven.

Mary's father always told her and Ken that if they dressed nicely—which, frankly, meant nicer than most people did—they would garner more respect. That wasn't always the case in school, where both were sometimes criticized for having their clothes picked out by their parents or, yet again, trying to show off, but by the time they'd graduated college, both saw that their father was right. And yet, Mary couldn't scorn anybody who dressed less formally than she did. Most likely they were dressing to be comfortable, or were just dressing as nicely as they could. Not everyone had a lot of money to spend on clothes, and even people who did often dressed casually. So while it was nice, at least in theory, to be shown additional respect, it would always bother Mary that she cared more about what other people thought than she wanted to or thought she should.

"That comes to seventy-nine seventeen," the cashier said to the woman standing in front of Mary. The woman smiled and cupped her left hand around her left ear. "I'm sorry. How much was that?"

"Seventy-nine seventeen," the cashier said, a little more loudly. There was no reason to announce it to anyone else.

And the lady opened a small change purse, carefully counted out her money, and then said, "I'm sorry, I only have seventy dollars with me."

The man standing behind Mary clicked his tongue, and Mary thought that was rude, even cruel. Again, thinking about the way the woman was dressed, Mary figured that she took whatever money she had around the house and hoped she wouldn't spend it all.

But the cashier was nice. "You're nine dollars and seventeen cents over. Is there something you'd like to put back?" she asked.

The woman smiled and said, "Not really," and for a moment Mary wondered if she was trying to convince the cashier to let her go, and make up the loss herself, the way Jesse had done for Mary two nights before. But she hated herself for thinking that the woman was playing a game; trying to get extra groceries for free. Especially as she saw that the woman was starting to shake.

So Mary said, "Excuse me," loudly, knowing that both the woman in front of her and the cashier would think she was going to complain about the holdup. But instead she said, "I have a spare ten on me. Please, just wrap up her groceries and take this," and she opened her own wallet, pulled out a ten dollar bill, leaned around the woman, and handed it to the cashier.

The woman's face collapsed, and she looked like she was about to cry. "Thank you," she said very quietly to Mary. "Thank you so very, very much. You're a good person."

Driving home, Mary wondered why she did that. The first thing to be said is that the woman didn't remind Mary of her mother; not at all. She was much older than her mother had been at the time she died, and the way she dressed and carried herself were different. Mary did think about her father, though, believing that he would have done the same thing. And, again, it wasn't for adulation. Mary had no desire to impress anybody, and, in fact, avoided looking at the cashier's face or saying anything when she checked out her own groceries, though that was usual for her. Nor did anybody say anything to her. No, she realized, she was trying to impress the judges, to show them, as the woman had said, what a "good" person she was, so she could get them in the habit of judging her positively. Because the thought of being judged negatively worried her, for the simple reason that she had no idea what the consequences might be. The benefit of being judged positively might not have seemed like a benefit at all, to many people, but Mary finally realized it was. And she doubted that any penalties would or could be as slight. On the other hand, she worried that the judges might see her act as manipulative; performed solely to curry their favor. Would that be held against her, or was that what the judges wanted, to exert enough of an influence so that Mary always did what they thought was "right"?

And yet, when she got home she saw no screen, no projector, and heard no whistle, then thought maybe it was because it was still daytime, and even with the curtains drawn, one couldn't see slides very well as long as it remained light outside. The judges, of course, were still sitting on the couch when she faced them, with the snow still falling and scattering, but they sat stock still; nothing moved. For fun she placed her hands in each of their chasms—she would no longer think of them as faces—and felt the warm, moist air blowing, which, she knew, meant they were thinking, and then turned around to play the piano.

She spent that afternoon playing Brahms. He wouldn't figure in her upcoming recital, but that was what she'd wanted to play when she'd first met the judges, and what she'd been going back to in the few days that followed. She chose one of his large, early works, the *Variations and Fugue on a Theme by Handel*, Op. 24.

INTERVIEWER: So what do you like so much about Brahms?

MARY: When you get over the sheer quality of his workmanship, which you need to do, because music, like much good art, affects one emotionally before it affects one mentally, though logic in construction brings its own emotional rewards, there's the nostalgia, which I love.

INTERVIEWER: So the sadness.

MARY: No, nostalgia isn't sadness. Nostalgia is a longing, a yearning for something you remember as having made you happy. So it's memory sweetened by hope. Sadness has no hope, it doesn't find happiness in memories or anything good, and after a while that can become off-putting. The only other composer I know whose music is as profoundly nostalgic as Brahms is Charles Ives. When I listen to his "craziness," the cacophony, the passages where three parts of an orchestra are playing three unrelated things simultaneously, I hear so much nostalgia, so much longing. Crazy, maybe, but I do. Listen to what each group is playing, and you'll hear what I mean. You want *sadness*, listen to Erik Satie. Nobody wrote sadder music than him.

INTERVIEWER: You're serious.

MARY: I'm telling you how I hear it. And it's not because I've been listening to Brahms and Ives and Satie for years and years. That's how their music struck me the first time I heard them, when I was in elementary school, and that's how their music strikes me now.

The *Handel Variations* wears its nostalgia more lightly than many of

Brahms' works, and not because it's relatively early, but if you listen carefully, you can hear it, just hiding itself sometimes. Mary had never performed the work publicly—it was lengthy, lasting almost half an hour without a pause, and taxing, as all of Brahms' piano music was, because Brahms had enormously long fingers and his hands could stretch, it's been claimed, up to twelve notes between his pinkies and his thumbs, but playing it then she decided to add it to one of her upcoming programs, though in tandem with the twentieth-century music that she favored.

For dinner that night, Mary drank a small glass of tomato juice, as she usually would, then ate some of the cucumber salad she'd prepared the night before, a salmon fillet grilled in lemon and butter, mashed potatoes, and green beans. She also drank a glass of lemonade, which she loved. She decided not to listen to music, and she didn't even call her friends, whom she hadn't spoken to in several days, though, again, they weren't always easy to reach on the weekend. Instead, she took a walk to Phoebe's, where she could be by herself with a cup of black coffee; very simple, very plain.

The fact that the judges wouldn't be judging her left her surprised and, frankly, disappointed, in part because she had nobody to discuss the incident in the supermarket with, including the judges themselves, who wouldn't be able to talk to her until, presumably, they found something more deserving of their attention. Ultimately, she decided that her decision was made only to validate herself, to convince herself that she was a good person, that she *mattered*, which was something she wished she could take for granted, and that, because it didn't involve anyone else, it wasn't worthy of being judged. But judgment, she thought, was often cast on people who committed similar acts. And, going to sleep, she told herself that even doing something to please God is a way of seeking validation.

If you ever asked Mary when things went awry between her and her brother, she wouldn't have been able to tell you. She might have said that they hadn't been especially close growing up, and that because the split occurred so gradually—even so naturally, as it must have felt at the time—she could never point to a day when things shifted from kinship to animosity. It hadn't been when Ken moved to Upstate New York, because by then he and Mary were barely talking to each other, which made his leaving easier for her and their parents. But after that they would see each other maybe once a year, she never saw Ken at any of her concerts, and she had performed in Binghamton twice, and phone calls became scarce. Unless he needed money, which, after a time, he always seemed to.

And yet, that following Wednesday night, less than a week after she'd been judged, and she hadn't been judged since, Ken called her at six o'clock, but Mary was eating dinner, and she thought he must have known that, so she ignored it. As usual, he left no message, but at nine-thirty that night, having listened to Brahms' Third Symphony and feeling satisfied, she called him back.

"Hey, Sis."

She was laying on her bed, but with her shoulders against the far side of the mattress, rather than on the pillows, which she used for resting her feet. She thought that if she let her head drop, more blood would flow to her brain, which would keep her more alert to, and make her more aware of, whatever Ken would tell her. So she would know better how to answer him.

"Ken. Hi," she said. She hated it when he called her "Sis," because that was the word her father used, when she was a child, to describe urine. She was sure Ken knew that. Or maybe he didn't. Mary, in common with a lot of people, couldn't always appreciate that not everyone knew exactly what she did. "I see you called, so I'm just returning the favor."

Ken laughed. "And isn't it just like you to return a favor, rather than provide one of your own."

She sighed loudly, for his benefit, or, rather, to solicit a reaction, and when there was none, she sighed again, even more loudly, but still got no reaction, and then, in the middle of her third and loudest sigh, they both broke into laughter. But she knew the laughter was forced, because she could always hear an edge in Ken's voice when he called. Still, one thing that always surprised Mary, when she spoke with or saw him, was how much more comfortable she felt than she expected to. Though only at first. And, as I've already pointed out, in her imagination Mary could idealize almost any situation.

"So what's up?" she asked, rousing herself and waiting for the inevitable. Ten...

"Well first I'd like to offer you my heartiest congratulations. I hear you're famous now. Or are about to be."

She laughed. She couldn't tell whether he was trying to sound affected— *heartiest?*—or whether that was the way he always spoke. She really didn't talk to him much. But not talking to him made her happy, so she replied cordially. "Well thanks, Ken. Not famous yet but, you know. Maybe some day." And fame still didn't inspire her. She wished she'd poured herself a glass of tomato juice, but knew the conversation wouldn't last long. She would grab a glass when she was done.

"But when that some day comes," Ken said, "I'll be able to point to you and say, 'That's my sister.'"

A trophy, she thought. Of course. How typical.

"And what does your upcoming schedule look like?"

Mary picked her head up. For a moment she wondered if he was asking her if they could get together, and was surprised by how much the thought appealed. "Well, I'm flying out to Iowa next week."

"Oh, Iowa. The big time," Ken said.

But Mary wouldn't let herself be baited. "It's a college, so maybe I can teach them something. We can *all* learn something, can't we, Ken?" She laughed half-heartedly. She wasn't looking forward to her trip overmuch.

"Maybe," Ken said. "Are you ever going to be in New York?"

She wasn't sure whether he meant the city or the state. She got up and lay down on her back with her head against the pillows. She decided her mattress was too firm. Clearly she'd been spoiled by mushy hotel mattresses. "Yes," she said, "I've got a recital at Weill Recital Hall in August."

"Who comes to New York in August? The heat."

"So I guess you won't be there," she said.

"Guess not," he said.

And suddenly Mary felt hurt, as though she'd just lost him. Or maybe just lost him again.

"You're appearing by yourself?"

"Yes," Mary said, feeling slightly numbed. "By myself. I always perform by myself."

INTERVIEWER: Do you like performing with an orchestra?

MARY: I don't.

INTERVIEWER: Why not?

MARY: For the same reason I don't like performing with a string quartet or a violinist or another pianist. When I make music I do it for myself, and I can't do that if there are other performers involved. One has to agree, compromise, integrate, compromise, ingratiate, compromise. It's not in me.

INTERVIEWER: But you have an audience to please. Isn't it the same thing?

MARY: Yes! It's *exactly* the same thing! Because I'm not trying to please an audience, I'm trying to please myself. No two people's life experiences are going to be the same, so what moves me won't necessarily move someone else, and vice versa. But don't think of an audience as a monolith; it's not. It's two thousand or so people, each hearing something completely different and being moved or transfixed or bored in different ways and for different reasons. The only time an audience acts as one is when someone starts applauding, and you know there has to be someone to start, and the other members, though maybe not all of them, join in. So for a few moments there's a commonality, and a lot of people like that. Just not me. Don't get me wrong, applause is wonderful, but it can also be very nullifying.

INTERVIEWER: How?

MARY: Well, sometimes, I'm convinced, I'd rather be sad because of what I'm thinking than happy because of what two thousand other people are thinking.

"So how are things with you?" Mary asked. She needed to change the subject.

There was a pause, and then he said, "Interesting."

Nine...

"Meaning what?" She stared at the ceiling.

"Well, as you must know by now, Ellora and I are no longer seeing each other."

How was she supposed to know that? She hadn't spoken to Ken in seven months. Unless he was implying that seven months was longer than he'd ever dated anyone, so she should have realized that he would have pushed whoever it was aside for someone else. Ellora was a biologist at Cornell University, and she lived a few miles outside of Ithaca, so, unlike Ken, she didn't have to drive more than an hour to and from work every day.

"What happened?"

"She said I didn't have enough time for her," Ken said.

But Mary knew what that meant. It wasn't because of his long daily commute or standing over his employees every minute of every day. It was, it had to have been, because he was seeing another woman.

"What's her name?" Mary asked.

"Who's name?"

"The new Ellora," Mary said.

Ken clicked his tongue, and Mary knew he was making fun of her. "Well, you see, that's just it. There *is* no new Ellora."

"Why not?" Mary asked, and then sat up and said quickly, "Don't get me wrong. I'm not saying there *should* be."

Ken sighed. "Because..."

Eight...

And she knew he was calling to ask for money. Which must have made perfect sense to him, because Ellora, who probably made more than he did, was no longer around.

Here was why he asked, with a little background thrown in for good measure. Mary and Ken, though born four years apart, looked exactly alike. If you saw them together you would think they were twins. Two faces carved by one sculptor with an extraordinarily limited imagination. But onstage, as I've said, Mary wore glasses, even though she didn't need them, and, as I've said, the lenses were clear, but I wonder if she did that not so much to stand out in people's minds as to differentiate herself from Ken, who didn't wear glasses. Also, Mary looked unquestionably Chinese while Ken looked unquestionably Indian. Mary's skin was golden yellow and smooth while Ken's skin was tannish and rutted. Which may be why Ken grew up hating what he called "the Chinese side of the family," particularly his mother and Mary. He saw them as different. Foreign. Not like him. And throughout his life he tried to endear himself to his father, though it was never clear to anyone in the family why that was, unless it was to validate his own ethnicity, which, let's be honest, wasn't the ethnicity of most of the people around him. In the end, though, Mary thought it was so that he could inherit their father's wealth when he died. Their father, a surgeon who had also inherited much from *his* father and invested extraordinarily well, was a very rich man. Only all of his money went to their mother, when he died, and then to Mary, not Ken, when she died, and Ken would never forgive any of them for it, alive or dead. Shortly thereafter he considered changing his name, but didn't, but the fact that Mary looked so much like him and had their father's last name must have been one reason, Mary thought, that Ken found her so hard to tolerate. Except for what money he thought she could give him, which he never believed was "hers," but which he could tolerate just fine.

"Well, Sis, I'll be honest. I'm hurting."

So phony.

"Over Ellora?"

"Over her, sure, but…"

"*But…*"

Seven…

Mary sighed, but she was irritated. She didn't like playing games. She knew what Ken wanted and just wished he could be straightforward enough to ask for it. That is until he asked. Then she would wish he hadn't. "What do you want, Ken?" She closed her eyes tightly, then opened them and shook her head.

"Have you ever noticed something, *Mary*?" He was wasting her time, but she heard the edge in his voice sharpen. "We use each other's names a lot when we talk to each other. I don't think people do that very often in real life."

"That's because this isn't real life, *Ken*. It's bad play, and I'm losing patience with it."

He laughed. "Oh, I thought we kept saying 'Mary' and 'Ken' to remind each other who we are, since we never see each other anymore."

And she could tell that he was losing patience with her. She yawned loudly. "So what, exactly, do you want?"

A deep breath.

Sixfivefourthreetwoonezero…

"Five thousand dollars would be nice, but if you can't afford it, I'll settle for twenty-five hundred."

Mary laid the phone down next to her, shut her eyes again, then picked it up and opened them. "You sound like someone who needs ten bucks for carfare but will *settle* for ten thousand because the poor asshole you're talking to is such a goddamned sucker."

"Mary, your language."

"Ken, your life."

"Can I have it? Please?"

"Ken, no," she said. "I can't give you five thousand dollars because I haven't got it."

"Look, as you know, I would normally ask Ellora—"

She stretched her shoulders. "I know. I understand. But Ellora's not there anymore."

"And you're the only one I have left."

She looked around her bedroom, her eyes alighting on her stereo equipment, her dresser, her chest, her mirror, and her headboard, all made of teak, and all very nice and very expensive, but then told herself that people who are well-off don't stay well-off by giving their money away.

"Ken, what do you need it for?" And asking what sounded like a sympathetic question actually made her feel more sympathetic.

"I have some debts I need to pay off."

That worried her, though, she thought, he must have wanted her to fret. "What kind of debts?"

Ken laughed, though genuinely. "The kind that need to be paid."

"Student loans?!" she asked. It couldn't have been.

"No."

She rubbed the index finger of her right hand against the right edge of her phone. "Ken, are you in trouble?" Meaning, was someone going to hurt him if he didn't pay up?

And after a moment Ken said "No," very quietly, as though he were ashamed that he couldn't give her a better answer.

But Mary was interested. "Ken, look. You have a good job, don't you? You're still running your business, aren't you?"

"Yes."

"Then where is your money going?" She thought he might be gambling, drinking, taking drugs, hiring women, hiring men. She had no idea, but as the possibilities started to build she became less and less interested, not because the possibilities themselves frightened or offended her, but because she didn't like thinking about her brother involved in those things. And that, she realized, was the biggest problem with not seeing or hearing from somebody for such a long time. He became frozen in her mind. She could only remember him as the man, or child, she once knew, and couldn't accept that his circumstances might have changed. "Ken, I'm sorry," she said genuinely, "I really am, but I can't."

"So that's your final word?"

"That's my final word."

And then, as she knew it would, the tone of the conversation changed. His voice became tight, piercing. And he yelled at her. "I have to ask you, cunt"—she hadn't heard that word in a long time—"because you have my money. You have the family fortune. Daddy didn't leave it to me, his son, the way he was supposed to." Mary and Ken both called their parents "mom" and "daddy," because they thought of their mother as distant and their father as approachable and giving.

"Ken, I'm your sister," she said, for lack of anything better to say.

And he said, "You're not my sister. You don't look like me." She did. "My father had sex with a real mahila before he found the gook bitch that had you. I'm surprised she didn't die from it. I bet you didn't know that daddy remarried before you were born." He didn't. "So you're not family."

And, of course, if she wasn't family, that was another reason she shouldn't have inherited the money. "Shit!" he said. "I should know better than to ask a goddamned chink for a buck. A fucking buck. A fuck-buck. Because they won't give it to you. They need it to fix up their homes or spend it on makeup or whatever the hell it is you fucking people do."

Mary felt her head grow tight and could imagine exploding in the kind of anger that had overtaken her brother, but she didn't because she was used to it, she'd heard it all before. Almost the same words, or maybe the exact same words. To Mary, Ken didn't have the creativity to sound threatening, and that, of all things, made her feel sorry for him.

That said, Mary couldn't turn away from Ken as easily as she could turn away from other people who would sometimes insult her—Mary was lucky because she was rarely subject to overt prejudice—because Ken could hurt her in a way strangers couldn't. He was familiar, and Mary liked thinking of familiarity as reassuring and comforting, not threatening.

"Daddy left his little girl all the money because he liked slants."

Mary said nothing, because nothing was the right thing to say. He was railing on because he wanted her to listen to him, to confess to herself more than to him that he deserved to be heard, that he meant something, that he meant something to her, that he could have some sort of hold on her. She knew that.

"He liked *slants*." Ken's favorite derisive term for Asians. "Did you hear me, Mary? He fucked mom because she was a slant. So tell me, Mary. Did daddy ever fuck *you*? He must have. You were young. You were pretty. Once. Or maybe not, Sis, because he probably couldn't find the way in."

Ken had told her many times that he thought she was a lesbian.

"So how did it feel, Mary? How did it feel to be fucked by daddy?!"

By then the hairs on the back of her neck were standing up. Because she loved her father, *their* father, and couldn't stand to hear him be disrespected like that. But all she did was move the phone away from her ear, take a deep breath, though at a distance, so he wouldn't hear it, and wait. She knew he was almost done. She expected, next, to hear him cry, but he wouldn't cry, not because he thought crying showed weakness—he didn't, and she'd seen him cry many times before—but because he was spent. When they were both children and Ken would fly into a rage, something that at first surprised her because neither of their parents ever yelled, she would get scared, but their father told her, "Some day even the sun is going to burn itself out." Though Mary would later wonder whether he'd said "the sun" or "the son."

Then, a little more quietly, he said, "Look, Sis, I work for my money, I don't pose and model in front of some fucking piano, like you, appealing to people who keep their heads stuck so far up their asses that they think every piece of shit they see is genius."

And after a pause, she asked flatly, "So tell me, Ken. How are things otherwise?"

And that seemed to defeat him, or what was left of him, and all Ken could say was, "There is no otherwise."

Then, after telling him she loved him, and hearing nothing in return, she hung up.

Big man in a small town, she thought. Big Man. BM. She laughed to herself and walked into the kitchen to pour herself a glass of tomato juice.

"Selman's Falls is so small," he once said, "it could have been made-up."

Standing at the sink, Mary wasn't sure how she felt. But she knew that she was right to not offer him any money, because she was sure she'd never see it again, and then she decided that he would never tell her what he needed it for, even if they were close, so what advantages could closeness between them bring? Thus, she was resolved to not offer Ken anything.

Mary walked into the living room. "Did you hear that?" she asked the judges. The question was rhetorical, of course, as the judges couldn't and wouldn't say anything to her unless they were going to pass judgment, but the whole conversation seemed so melodramatic and ridiculous that she felt like prolonging the theatrics. That said, she thought she saw the left shoulder of the third judge move, but decided she was imagining it because, maybe, she wanted to talk to them again.

But rather than talk to them, she decided to call Leila. Leila had known both of Mary's parents and Ken. She could never believe how quiet Mary's family was (usually). Having dinner with the four of them one night, she was amazed that no one at the table raised his or her voice, but no one in Mary's family, Mary told her, ever did. Except, of course, for Ken, but he never yelled in front of strangers.

"If no one in my family raised their voice," Leila said, "I'd get my hearing checked."

Leila, she knew, didn't like Ken. More than any of her other friends, but that was because Leila, being her closest friend, saw Ken more than her other friends did. She found him a sycophant. The year before, having just read a biography of Joseph Goebbels, she told Mary, "Goebbels was the ultimate yes-man. Like your brother. He worshipped Hitler and, so, was blinded by him. Everything Hitler did was right, brilliant, perfect. He could find no fault with him. Do you know what he named his six children? Goebbels, I mean, not Hitler, who didn't have any kids. Helga, Heidrun, Holdine, Hildegard, Hedwig, and Helmut. All starting with an 'H,' no doubt out of deference to the Führer, though that's been debated. Now don't get me wrong, I'm not saying that Ken is any Joseph Goebbels; he isn't, he couldn't be. But there's that same slimy insincere ingratiation."

So maybe that was why Mary wanted to talk to her. To convince herself that she'd done the right thing, made the right decision—and it was a decision, not an inevitability; she knew that—to not help her brother. And Leila, more than anyone else, would legitimize that.

Mary walked back into her bedroom and sprawled out on her bed. Calling Leila, she remembered the conversation they'd had after she won her competition, and she felt dreamily satisfied.

Leila answered. "Hello?"

"Hey, Leila, it's me," Mary said.

"Hello?" Leila repeated, after a pause.

"Leila, it's me. Mary."

"Is there someone on the phone?" Leila asked.

Mary pulled the phone away from her ear and shook her head. Bringing it next to her, she said, "Wait, I'll call you back. We must have a bad connection." She hung up, not surprised, because sometimes in the late spring and summer the phone lines in Ardell were jammed.

"Hello?" Leila said, and immediately Mary could hear that the connection was better.

"Hey, it's me," Mary said.

And after a moment Leila asked, "'Me' who?"

Mary laughed. "Mary," she said. She laughed again. "Since when have you become a practical joker? I could see that happening with Lizzy before you."

"How do you know Lizzy?" Leila asked, sounding angry and threatened.

"What do you mean, how do I know Lizzy? We roomed together at school." Mary looked around her to make sure she was where she thought she was. "Why am I telling you this? Leila, what's going on?"

"Who *is* this?" Leila asked again, but that time sounding more frightened than angry.

"It's Mary. Mary Sorabi."

And after a pause, Leila said, "You must have the wrong number," and hung up.

Impressive, Mary thought. Leila was playing a game but she made it sound convincing. So she figured she'd wait a few minutes then call her again.

"Hello?" Leila said.

And Mary was sure she could hear the difference in Leila's voice. Calmer, more relaxed. More centered. And Leila could tell, by looking at her phone, that it was the same person who was calling. If she didn't want to hear from her, or was afraid, she just wouldn't have answered. "Okay, time for the fun and games to be over. It's me and—"

And then Leila started screaming. "Look, I don't know who the fuck you are, I don't know any Mary Whatever-the-Hell-Your-Name-Is, and I'm going to tell you one more time to leave me the fuck alone, or I'm going to report you to the police!" And she hung up.

Mary ran out into the living room, breathing so hard she could barely catch her breath. "What happened?! What the fuck happened to Leila?!" she asked. And hearing the horrible whistle again, she knew the judges had made a decision. Which both scared her and, paradoxically, calmed her down, because then, at least, there would be a discussion.

The first judge turned his head slightly to look at the second judge, and then said, "Nothing happened to Leila. What *happened*, happened to you. Leila isn't our concern, you are. Mary, please sit down," he said, and graciously pointed to the piano bench on which she always sat when she spoke with them or, as she thought of it, semi-humorously, when they held court. "Mary, Leila doesn't know who you are anymore. You've been forgotten."

"Forgotten? Me?!"

"Yes," the first judge said. "You. Do you know why?"

"No! Of course I don't know why," Mary said, and she could feel her heart beating so hard it was vibrating in her throat. She kept her mouth open because she couldn't breathe any other way.

The second judge leaned forward. "Because you lost. You lost, Mary. And nobody remembers who loses a competition, they only remember who wins."

And the third judge said, "Think about it, and you'll realize that that's perfectly logical. It makes perfect sense."

Then Mary screamed, "But this isn't a competition. It's a judgment! They're two completely different things!"

"That's right," the first judge said, "they are. And, as we said before, we're here neither to help you nor to hurt you. Only to judge you. And, once again, you've been judged."

INTERVIEWER: So what do you think of judging in general?

MARY: That's a good question.

INTERVIEWER: Thank you.

MARY: By which I mean, I have a good answer. Or *think* I have a good answer. So don't think I'm complimenting you. (*Laughs*) Do you mean in the musical world?

INTERVIEWER: Yes.

MARY: I think it's skewed. Okay, there's legal judgment. And that makes sense to me. A defendant is brought in front of a jury who judges him or her, but against a proscribed law. If the person broke it, he or she is found guilty. If he or she respected it, he or she is found innocent. Ideally. But what kind of proscribed law applies to a piano competition? The closest thing I can think of is making sure the person played the music without hitting any wrong notes. But look at all the live performances that are full of wrong notes, and people *love* them because they get so emotionally caught up in the performance. So you're judging against someone's very subjective criteria that can't be called right or wrong. It's like composers who tried to write like Beethoven or Wagner or Schoenberg. Many of them were failures, because you couldn't apply what worked for one person to anyone else. So same thing here. You can't apply legal judgment to a musician.

"Can we have the projector, please?" the first judge asked.

The light in the brass lamp went out and Mary again saw the projection screen and slide projector, with the little felt cups around its feet, on the cocktail table.

"Mary, please relax," the second judge said. "This one is going to take a while. And don't worry. All of the ramifications of being forgotten will be explained to you."

"As well as the possible advantages," the third judge said, pushing his shoulders against the backrest.

"First slide, please," the first judge said. And Mary saw the outside of Ken's house. "Exhibit A, the home of Ken Sorabi. Which is located at number 8709 Bath Avenue, Selman's Falls, New York. What do you think of it, Mary?"

The slide showed a small, white clapboard house sitting on an acre of land surrounded by forest. The first thing Mary noticed was how small the house was, and the fact that the small house, sitting amidst the large stretch of land, didn't take on the significance or even the monumentality of the area around it, the way, she suddenly thought, paintings did in museums. But maybe that was because there was nothing extraordinary about the house itself. It looked very simple, very plain.

"I don't know what to say," Mary said.

"You're familiar with it, aren't you?" the first judge asked.

"Well, of course I am. I've been there. Once."

"How long ago was that?" the third judge asked.

"When he first bought it, so, maybe ten years ago? I don't remember." She sounded flustered, but she was just annoyed with her own faulty memory.

"But not since," the first judge said.

Mary shook her head nervously, but she was calming down. "No," she said. "Not since." And then, rousing herself, she said, "You know, the thing that strikes me about it is...how small it is. Are you sure you have the right house?"

The first judge nodded. "We have the right house."

"And I remembered it being closer to the lake. To Seneca Lake. Or, no, I'm sorry. Cayuga Lake."

"Is that what you remember?"

"I think so," Mary said. Then, "Yes, that's exactly what I remember. I've been there, and...yes. His house was right on the lake....Wasn't it? It must have been. Right?"

MARY: You know what my harmony professor at Curtis once said? Seriously. He said that you can never unlock the secrets of Schoenberg's music because it's atonal, so it has no key. Which is funny and, technically, true but, sadly, misses the point completely.

INTERVIEWER: What's the point?

MARY: The point is that his music is expressive. Profoundly expressive, deeply expressive, even hyper-expressive, but people don't believe that because they don't expect it to be. The average listener listens to Schoenberg and finds his music ugly because he or she expects it to sound that way. Because he or she has been told that it *is* ugly. And most people don't hear what's in front of them, they hear what's in their minds. They're so convinced that what they're going to be "assaulted with"—I've actually heard that—is going to be so terrible that the slightest unkind thing they hear has them applauding themselves and saying, "See? I'm right! It *is* awful," and anything that might be beautiful, or nice, or at least not ugly, is just dismissed as an anomaly. They need to get outside of their own minds and hear what's in front of them.

"The lake is a short walk from his house," the third judge said, "but his property doesn't abut it."

"No," the first judge said. "It's not like your house."

Mary breathed in and out deeply and shook her head.

"Was this your parents' house?" the second judge asked.

"No," Mary said, and smiled embarrassedly. "It has only two bedrooms."

"I wouldn't use the word 'only' to describe anything about this house," the third judge said.

"Next slide, please, Mr. Slide-Advancer," the first judge said. "Let's take a look inside."

And Mary saw a picture of Ken and Ellora sitting at his kitchen table, sipping coffee and smiling at each other. Or, rather, Ellora was smiling at Ken; Ken's face was turned slightly away. Their hands were extended but only their index fingers touched.

"He must have had something on his mind," the third judge said.

"Do you think he loves her?" the first judge asked.

And Mary was surprised to hear herself answer, "As much as he can."

But, she thought to herself, he can never love anybody enough.

Ellora wasn't, Mary thought, traditionally beautiful, or even good-looking. She was short and stocky, so very much unlike Ken, who was tall and thin, wore her dark brown hair combed back, which accentuated her very high forehead, like her friend Julietta, and had extremely small teeth. But her smile held its own allure, and Mary felt sorry she'd never met her.

"Next slide please, Mr. Slide-Advancer."

And this went on for thirty more slides. Mary, of course, was in none of them. Did she wish she were? She wasn't sure.

"The argument *for*, please," the first judge said.

"The argument *for* giving Ken the money," the third judge said, looking at Mary, "is that he needs it more than you do. Or, perhaps it would be more accurate and more fair to say that he could profit from it more than you can."

"The argument *against*, please," the first judge said.

"The argument *against* giving Ken the money," the second judge said, "is that Ken would spend it on illegal or at least legally questionable materials."

"But no such materials have been presented to us, have they?" the first judge asked.

The second judge shook his head, and the third judge said, "They have not."

"So here's what we decided," the first judge said. "You were presented with another choice, just as you had been the first time. The first time it was whether to tip Jesse the five dollars for the additional chicken wings he brought you. This time it was whether to lend Ken the five thousand dollars he asked for."

Mary said, "'Lend' is not the right—"

"Mary, please," the first judge said. "I'm speaking. You'll have plenty of time to ask your own questions and answer ours when we're through." But he sounded downright avuncular, and that lack of reprimand in his voice made her chastise herself, passing her own judgment, as it were.

"I'm sorry," Mary said.

The second judge shook his head. "No need to apologize. Please continue."

And Mary wasn't sure whether he was talking to the first judge or to her.

But then the first judge said, "Ken is not a wealthy man. He owns and runs his own company, yes, but he doesn't make the kind of living you might expect him to. You understand that, don't you?"

"Of course," Mary said, but she could barely speak. "What kind of trial is this?"

"Mary," the second judge said consolingly. "You're being judged, you're not on trial."

"What's the difference?" Mary asked.

The first judge sighed. "In a trial," he said, "you can defend yourself."

"Can I get up for a moment?" Mary asked.

"Please," the second judge said.

Mary walked over to the recliner, sat down, and cried. And when she was done she walked back to the piano bench, straightened her skirt, and realized, surprisingly, that she couldn't tell what she was crying about. It could have been that she missed Ken, that she thought she'd actually wronged him, that she felt and hated her lack of control with the judges watching over her, or maybe it was all of those things, or maybe it was none.

"The bottom line," the first judge said, "is that Ken needs that money more than you do." Mary simply stared at him. Then he said, "You can speak now."

"Okay," she said, straightening her skirt once more. "I'm not denying that he needs the money." In fact, she'd been denying it pretty vehemently. "But I'm just not sure why. I'm not sure where his money is going."

The third judge shook his head, and the second judge said, "Maybe it's not going anywhere. Maybe it's not going because there isn't much of it to go."

And Mary admitted that she hadn't thought of that. She'd just made assumptions about Ken based on what was actually very little concrete information.

"So, as a result," the first judge said, "you've been forgotten."

"So, in other words, I cease to exist," Mary said.

"Oh, no!" the second judge said, looking like he was going to jump up.

"Those are two very different things."

"Though some people don't realize that," the third judge said.

"True," said the first judge, and Mary's mouth formed the same word. "Look in your wallet. Please."

Mary, who always carried her wallet with her, extracted it from her skirt pocket and began counting her money, which was the same amount she remembered having since getting back from Phoebe's the Saturday night before. She looked quizzically at the judges, who shook their heads, not understanding why she didn't realize what they were asking her to do.

"You still have your driver's license, Mary," the first judge said. "You still have your credit cards. You haven't ceased to exist. Not at all."

Mary looked at her driver's license and looked at her credit cards, checking her name and their numbers, and everything seemed to be in order.

"And you still have your bank account," the third judge said, "but try walking into your bank and see if the teller who usually waits on you remembers you. He or she won't."

"To be remembered again," the first judge said, "all you have to do is win the next competition."

"Or win our favor," the third judge said.

"But think about how badly you want to. Both win our favor and be remembered. And realize that being remembered and existing are not the same thing."

"I'm surprised she didn't understand that," the second judge said quietly to the others.

"So about the advantages," the first judge said, and the other two judges said, "Yes."

"The first and most obvious advantage to being forgotten, in your case, is that Ken won't know who you are," the second judge said.

And the third judge added, "So he won't be asking you for money."

"Then I don't exist," Mary said.

The first judge put his right palm forward. "Oh, you very much do exist. You're just...well," he shrugged, "the sister he never knew he had."

"And there are other, perhaps less obvious 'advantages'" the third judge said, leaning back.

Then the second judge said, "Among which are not hearing from people you don't want to hear from. Which would be especially nice for someone who enjoys her solitude as much as—"

But Mary had turned her face toward the recliner and asked irately, "Why are you criticizing me again?"

The first judge threw his arms behind him, hitting the backrest, however lightly, and when Mary turned to look at them to see what made that noise, he said, "Mary, for the second time, we're not criticizing you." But calmly.

"You already told us once that we were criticizing you for that," the third judge said, "and we're not and weren't. And the second time is no more charming than the first time. Now the *third* time, maybe...."

"Mary," the first judge said, "to repeat, you have a good life. A wonderful life. A rare life. Don't lose it and don't lose sight of it. We're not criticizing you for that."

"You must criticize yourself for it a lot," the second judge said, and Mary agreed that she did. All the time.

The first judge crossed his arms, crossed his legs, and leaned back. "Mary, let me ask you a question that, I think, will help you understand us better."

Mary flattened her lips and said, "Sure."

"When you decided not to give Ken the money, did you feel guilty?"

The second judge shook his head. "There is no right answer. Only an honest one."

Mary pursed her lips. "No," she said. "No. I didn't." She leaned back.

"We felt it," the third judge said. "Which means you must have felt it, too."

"Right," the second judge said. "We feel it; why can't you?"

"She's not being honest," the first judge said in a clear voice that sounded higher in pitch than usual.

"Just because you feel some way doesn't make it right," Mary said, crossing her arms, something she almost never did, because she thought it was childish, "and just because you say something doesn't mean I have to agree with you."

"True," the first judge said, nodding. "But...," he said, and held out his right palm facing downward.

What the first judge wanted to explain, but chose not to, was that she wouldn't have been agreeing with them; *they*'d already agreed with *her*. She really did feel guilty, but couldn't—or didn't want to—admit it to herself. And therein lay the problem. People who like to think of themselves as independent, the way Mary did, will often disagree with someone who feels the same way, just for the sake of being different and, well, independent.

"It's all right," the second judge said, and shifted slightly to the left and the right, then rested his palms on his thighs.

"If it's all right with you, Mary," the first judge said, "we'd like to ask you about your family."

And Mary's mood brightened, because she thought that if she could explain what her family was like and what they meant or, occasionally, didn't mean to her, the judges might reverse their decision. At that time Mary was concerned about being forgotten.

The first judge wrapped his left arm around the back of his neck. "Who's child are you, Mary? Your mother's child or your father's child?"

"Which is to say," the second judge said, "Who do you take after? Your mother or your father?"

Mary smiled. "Well, I look like my mother," she said, "but I think I take after my father."

"Let's start with your mother," the first judge said. "Tell us a little about her."

"But please understand, Mary," the second judge said, leaning forward, "we base all of our judgments on facts, not motives."

"I understand," Mary said, and smiled again, but to cover her disappointment at realizing that no, the judge's decision couldn't be reversed. "It's interesting that you should ask me about her, though, because the interviewer asked me about her too, which I found very strange."

INTERVIEWER: Tell me about your mother.

MARY: My mother?! (*Pause*) My mother? Well, all right. Though I'm not going to ask what you want to know, because I'm going to tell you what I want to tell you. Mom's name was Margaret, and her maiden name was Leung, so Margaret Leung. And for a while she wanted to change it to *Long*, but she was so obviously Chinese that she worried people would ask, "What kind of name is *Long* for a Chinese woman?" And people knew that she wasn't married, so she couldn't tell them that it was her married name. She looked like somebody whose name could be Leung. But she felt that she couldn't fit in, except with other Chinese. So she didn't bother, and all of her friends were from Chinatown, just the way she was. Even after she moved to New Jersey, the only friends she had were her friends from her old neighborhood.

INTERVIEWER: So she gave up. On trying to fit in, I mean.

MARY: No, she just didn't bother. My mother never "gave up" on anything.

INTERVIEWER: Did she think it was important to fit in?

MARY: She must have. She was an extremely timid woman.

INTERVIEWER: And deep down inside, everybody wants to fit in, don't they?

MARY (*Yelling*): No! Get out of your mind the stupid idea, and yes, I'm going to call it that, that everybody wants to fit in. (*Laughs*) My God, If everybody wanted to fit in, there'd be no audience at classical music concerts.

"Well, she was a sweet woman," Mary said. "Very giving, very loving, in her way, but very sad."

"Sad in what way?" the third judge asked, crossing his legs.

And Mary smiled, suddenly realizing that there were many ways to be sad. "Well," she said, and let out a deep breath, which surprised her, "not much seemed to make her happy. Or, I don't know, maybe it did, but she never expressed her emotions openly."

"Then what makes you think she was sad?" the second judge asked.

"Maybe the fact that she didn't smile," Mary said. "At least when I was growing up." Mary didn't often like talking about her childhood, because when she talked about it she needed to bring herself back to it, to remember what it was like, and that left her feeling as vulnerable as she'd felt then. "Friends would come over, relatives would visit a lot, but she always complained that she had nothing to do and nothing to look forward to. Or, if something did make her happy, the happiness would never last. She could acknowledge that she'd been happy three hours ago, but wasn't happy then."

"What did she look like?" the first judge said, turning his head to the pictures of Brahms and Schumann behind the piano.

"She was a small woman," Mary said. "Maybe five-foot-two or five-foot-three. But her hairdo was enormous." She laughed. "It practically obscured her face and took up more room than her head, or so it seemed. Her eyes were small, her mouth was small and withdrawn. My father once told me that she looked like she sucked on alum. And she always wore clothes that were too big for her, maybe to make her appear larger, but they only made her look smaller when you saw the contrast."

"You don't have any pictures of her here," the first judge said, looking around.

"I don't have pictures of anyone in my family," Mary said, dipping her head slightly because she thought she was supposed to feel guilty for that.

"Anything else?" the third judge asked. "Any funny stories?"

And again Mary wondered who, exactly, they were. She'd *known* them, if that was the right word for it, for less than a week but felt as though she'd known them all her life. "Can I ask you a question?" Mary lifted her head slightly.

"Of course," the second judge said.

"How old are you?"

The third judge cleared his throat. Then the first judge said, "We're as old as the world, Mary, and as young as you are."

"Please don't speak in riddles," Mary said, and was surprised that she'd said "Please."

"Were we speaking in riddles?" the second judge asked. "Think about it, and you'll realize that we're not. I think we answered your question exactly."

"So a story about her," Mary said, a dreamy expression coming over her face. "Okay, but it's not funny. I think my mother was the loneliest person I ever knew. She had a big family, which was good to her, and a lot of friends, but, as I said, she was never happy. Toward the end of her life she started talking to her medication." She giggled. "I'm sorry, I'm not saying that to be funny. But she'd take a container of pills, and she was taking a lot of pills because she had cervical cancer, and when she'd tip the container into her left palm and two pills or capsules would come out at the same time, maybe because they were stuck together, she would separate them, place one back with her long fingers, and say, 'Sorry, not today, sweetheart. Maybe tomorrow.' She was so lonely that she had to make the inanimate objects around her into her friends, or at least her companions."

"How did that make you feel?" the second judge asked.

"It broke my heart," Mary said.

"Why?" the first judge asked, and leaned to the left.

"Why?" Mary repeated. "Because I hated seeing how sad she was."

The three judges faced each other and seemed to whisper. Then they faced her again.

"It's interesting that you should say you hated *seeing* how sad she was," the first judge said, "rather than that you hated the fact that she *was* sad. There's an important difference there, Mary. This wasn't about you. But you never realized that, did you?"

And Mary started to cry again.

"Why the tears, Mary?" the second judge asked sympathetically.

"Because I miss her," Mary said.

Then the third judge leaned forward and said, "And maybe for the right reasons."

"So now tell us about your father," the first judge said. Did he know that would get Mary to smile?

"He was just the opposite," she said, "And I was jealous of him." She laughed, as though she'd just realized that, by saying it. "He was always so happy, and I wanted to know his secret. Well, for the longest time I did."

INTERVIEWER: Are you jealous of people who have more than you do?

MARY: I don't know, because I don't know anyone who has *more* than I do. They have different things than I do. Is that something to get jealous about? Maybe. If it's something I want, but usually no. You know, I think there's this list of things that we're all supposed to want and get jealous over if we don't have. But that's ridiculous, because we don't all want the same things. It's like asking me if I'm jealous of people who play Beethoven better than I do. No, I'm not, because I don't like Beethoven, so I don't care. And I think I'm better off that way.

"Did you ever find it out?" the second judge asked. "What his secret was?"

"I think I did," Mary said. "He kept a distance from most other people. He never got really involved in other people's lives, so maybe he didn't pick up whatever pain they were suffering, and absorb that the way my mother did. But you have to understand, there are two reasons, broadly speaking, that people stay away from each other. One is fear. What they call 'fear of closeness.' But it's real. The other reason, though, is satiety. Or satisfaction. Staying away from somebody simply because he or she doesn't make you as happy as you make yourself."

"So people *can* make themselves happy," the first judge said. "A lot of people don't believe that."

Mary looked down. "My mother never believed that. That's why she was around other people all the time," she said. "To get something she didn't think she could get from herself. Although she never did. And that, I guess, was why she always pushed us, my brother, and I—"

"You can call him Ken," the second judge said.

"Why she wanted Ken and I to make a lot of friends. So we could be happy. It worked for Ken, but it didn't work for me."

"What did your mother say about that?" the third judge asked.

"She didn't say much, but I don't think she approved."

"And your father?" the second judge asked.

Mary laughed. "He defended me. He always told me, 'Don't let an unhappy person tell you how to be happy.'"

"Is there anything else you'd like to tell us about him?" the second judge asked. He shrugged and turned his palms up.

Mary sat forward, straightened her blouse, and pursed her lips. "Well, sure," she said. "My father was a very even-tempered man. He never lost his temper because he had no temper to lose." She glanced at the ceiling for a moment then tried to hide a smile. "No, actually the one thing that drove him crazy was trying to tear plastic." She laughed. "If you can believe it. He hated unwrapping anything sealed in plastic, which could be one reason why he bought himself so little. As a scientist he understood it. Plastics are made up of huge molecules. Water, he would explain, has only three atoms, two of hydrogen and one of oxygen, but plastics have tens of thousands of atoms, so the molecules themselves are physically hard to break. So you should see him trying to unwrap something. 'Oh my damn!' 'Goddamn it!' 'Damn it all to hell!' 'Surely this is a joke of...' one or another higher power. But then he'd laugh, break into his high-pitched, hooty giggle, reach for a pair of scissors, and everything would be all right again." She shook her head. "God, how I miss him." And after a pause, "One thing I should say, though, is that my father had a funny idea on pain and suffering. He believed that everyone receives an allotment of pain at birth, but how it's distributed depends on what the person does with his or her life. So when, for instance, Ken, who was nine, fell on the sidewalk and scraped his knee and began to cry, my father told him that it was just a minor disruption. That it could have been something much worse but wasn't. Now that might sound terribly unsympathetic, and I'm sure Ken thought it was, and don't get me wrong, my father took care of it, but he thought that it was a sort of payment, maybe hush money, you could say, so that something more terrible wouldn't happen. In other words, I think my father believed that your allotment of pain and suffering could be divided among numerous little inconveniences—well, I'm sure any child would think a scraped knee is more than an inconvenience—or a few colossal misfortunes. And he, of course, my father, preferred dealing with the numerous inconveniences, which I think was how he remained as upbeat as he did."

"Was your father a religious man?" the third judge asked.

Mary shook her head. "Not at all. At least not in the conventional sense. The day he married my mother was the last time he stepped into a church."

"Until he died," the first judge said.

"Until he died," Mary repeated.

"How did he explain death to his patients' parents?" asked the second judge.

"I don't know," Mary said. "I don't know that he ever lost a patient. If he did, he never told us about it. You know, the doctor-patient relationship."

"Privacy," said the first judge, and the other two nodded.

"But what was wrong with his philosophy was that when things went well for him, he started to panic. I could see that. It made him uneasy, because he was sure that he would pay for it in some way or other. Like every action having an equal and opposite reaction."

The third judge cleared his throat. "So he didn't enjoy being happy," he said.

Mary shook her head. "Sometimes I don't think he felt he was entitled to it. But after a while he went with it and could be happy again."

The first judge stretched his shoulders. "Please tell us about your brother."

Mary threw her head back and laughed. "Do you want to know why he was named Ken?" She was still thinking about her father. "Because, when he was born, my father said he looked like a Ken doll. And he did grow up to be tall and thin, and, to some people, not me, handsome. And when he was in high school he used to walk through the halls robotically, and when someone would ask him why he was walking like that, he'd say, 'Because my name is Ken Dahl.' That was when he had a sense of humor."

The third judge craned his neck. "He doesn't have a sense of humor now?"

Mary slouched. "Oh, I'm sure he does. In a way. But he's a very tense man. Not like my father. Not given to enjoying life. Worrying? Yes, of course. All the time. But enjoying life? No, I don't think so."

"You think he's abusive," the first judge said.

Mary leaned forward. "You heard what he said to me. You must know." She no longer thought that anything happened or could happen in her life without the judges being aware of it. And then, on a lark, she asked, "If I continue to lose, will my face disappear?" And although she asked the question lightly, hearing herself ask it made her concerned.

"Like ours?" the second judge asked. "No. We've never been judged."

The third judge cleared his throat and crossed his legs. "Mary, we'd like to ask you one more question about Ken. Has he ever threatened you? Say, with bodily harm?"

"Or hurt you physically?" the second judge asked.

Mary tightened her lips and leaned back against the piano, but it remained mute. "No, but there are other ways of hurting someone."

"Of course there are," the first judge said. "But...and please don't take this the wrong way...."

Mary hated it when people said that because she knew that whatever was going to follow would naturally be taken the wrong way, assuming that the wrong way was hurtful.

"Do you love him?"

She looked shocked. "Ken? Yeah, I guess so."

"Why?" the first judge asked.

"Why?" Mary asked, stiffening her upper body. "I really don't know. I *shouldn't*—"

"Then I'll tell you why," the second judge said, raising the index finger of his right hand. "It's instinct. That's what holds families together. Instinct, not logic."

"Logically," the third judge said, leaning forward, "it could be argued that you and Ken shouldn't get along at all. But you do. In your own way."

"Logic isn't what's kept animals alive for longer than people have been here," the second judge said.

"And that's why decisions are never really difficult," the first judge said, leaning forward to straighten his pants. He picked his head up. "As you yourself said. Because good judgment is based on instinct. Decisions become difficult only when you complicate them with logic."

"Mary," the first judge said, crossing his arms and sitting back. "Have you ever been the victim of prejudice?"

"No," Mary said quickly, and shook her head.

"Never?" the third judge asked.

"Well," Mary said hesitantly.

"Well?" the first judge asked.

Mary sighed.

INTERVIEWER: What kind of prejudice have you encountered? Have you ever been called a "gook" or a "slant"?

Now here I have to interject. I can't imagine that any interviewer in his right mind (or what passes for such) would ask someone that question, unless he was trying to bait her. And why would he? That would corrupt the point of the whole interview unless, again, it was done as a ruse. But it's in the transcript, and as there are no interruptions or intercalations included, we have to assume that, at one point at least, it was edited from the original recording, a copy of which (or even the original) I do not have. So I have to believe that it actually was said.

MARY: What the fuck kind of question is that?

INTERVIEWER: As I said before, the type that warrants an answer. Understand, Mary, my readers want to know everything they can about the people I write about, the people I interview. Your background informs your foreground. You know that. It makes you who you are, and without knowing that, without an awareness of what came before, no one can know who you are.

MARY: Bullshit. They can look at me, hear me play, talk to me, and they'll know enough.

INTERVIEWER: Will they?

"I can tell you a story about prejudice, but it didn't happen to me directly."

"Okay," the first judge said, sounding intrigued.

"My mother was an excellent cook," Mary said, "and she didn't cook only Chinese food, as you might have thought if you'd known her. She 'indulged,' as she liked to say, in Indian cooking, and loved the fragrance, delicacy, and floral notes of so many of the Indian spices. In fact, *interestingly*, I think she loved the sound of Hindi, too. Less harsh than Mandarin, which was what she spoke. Anyway, she made a dish, chicken vindaloo served with aloo palak, you know, something simple, for one of our neighbors one night; a woman named Pearl. Not a close neighbor, relatively speaking. She lived next door but we almost never talked to her. But Pearl had just lost her husband, well, a few months earlier, and my mother decided to cook her something, to be nice, having waited long enough after the hubbub had died down."

"A few months sounds like long enough," the second judge said, nodding.

"But the next day, the day after my mother brought the food to Pearl, our neighbor on the other side, with whom we were closer, told my mother that Pearl said she couldn't eat it, because she was afraid that 'the Indian spices' would stain her silverware. When my father found out about that, he laughed. 'Her mind is already stained,' he said. 'Why is she worrying about her silverware?' But that was the kind of man my father was. Always forgiving."

"How did your mother take it?" the first judge asked.

"She took it well, I guess," Mary said. "Because she never cooked anything for Pearl again, nor, do I think, she ever said another word to her."

"That *was* taking it well," the second judge said, nodding. "She could have overlooked it, as your father did, but why bother, when somebody did something wrong and justice needed to be meted out?"

"Retribution," the third judge said.

Mary looked thoughtful for a moment, then said, "I hate to think what Ken would have made of it. I don't think he ever knew. I don't think he would have cared. He was still living with us then."

"Ken, yes," the third judge said. "The man who threatens you."

"Oh, Mary, where are our manners?" the first judge asked, pretending to sound playful, but Mary heard what she thought was mockery in his voice. "Would you like a drink?"

The question suddenly irritated her, but she didn't know whether it was because she was scared, because she'd already decided that he was making fun of her, or because of the absurdity of the situation. She rubbed her teeth together. "This is *my* house," she said. She liked the feeling of control; the feeling that a guest never has, which was ironic, because she would almost always see her friends at their houses rather than invite her friends to hers.

The third judge lurched forward and said, "Oh, we're not offering you anything. We just want you to know that if you want something, we won't stop you."

And that got her even more irritated. She felt her throat get tight and she breathed out heavily, opening and closing her fists. Then she yelled, "Look!"

At which moment the third judge lifted himself up slightly, pointed at her and yelled back, "See! Do you see it?!" He turned to the other judges. "She's angry! Mary, you're angry. We can see it. We can feel it. But think about it. You shouldn't be. Because what I've just done—telling you that you can do whatever you want, letting you know that we won't stop you, that we *can't* stop you, is given you all the control." He shook his head. "Just without its usual trappings of power."

The second judge laughed, but not derisively. "Understand, when it comes to Ken, that you have more control than he does. Ken can hurt you, but he can't hurt you as much as you can hurt yourself."

And at that Mary laughed back, suddenly relaxing and shaking her head. "Clever, Detective Porfiry. Very clever."

"Mary," the first judge said, leaning forward, "one more question on Ken, then we'll let it drop. Do you think he would defend you if he knew you were the victim of prejudice?"

Mary stuck out her chin and said, "You know, I have no idea if he would. I guess so. He berates me for being Chinese, or *looking* Chinese, I should say, because he's every bit as much Chinese as I am," And then she stopped, shook her head, and said, "And yes. I think he would defend me, because of what I just said."

Though Mary, of course, could be subject to other kinds of prejudice—because she was a woman, because she was half-Indian, because she was Catholic, or at least raised Catholic, because she was unmarried, because she didn't have sex, because she was intelligent, because she played classical music; the list could be expanded limitlessly—but she seemed most sensitive about her Chinese heritage, maybe because that was what Ken held most strongly against her.

"I think we've said enough for tonight," the first judge said, stretching his arms in front of him, and for a moment Mary expected to see him yawn.

"But wait," she said, "I still have more questions."

"On what?" the third judge asked.

"You said that things will return to normal, that I'll be remembered again, after you make your next positive decision about me."

"After we pass our next positive judgment, yes," the first judge said, and nodded slowly.

And the third judge quickly leaned forward to say, "Again, I wouldn't read too much into the word 'positive.'"

"But remember what it all means, and think hard, Mary, about how much you really want to be remembered," the second judge said.

"But when are you going to make that decision?" Mary asked, but didn't like the way the question sounded. Too needy, too plaintive. So she said, "And I ask that because it's obvious that you *don't* judge me on everything."

"How so?" the first judge asked, leaning forward himself.

"The woman I helped in the supermarket last weekend." She felt her heart beating too quickly. "Why didn't you judge me on that?"

The first judge leaned back and rested his arms on the top of the backrest. "We did. As we explained, we judge you on everything. But, in essence, we judge you twice. Sometimes. First we look at what you did and decide whether we want to come to a positive or negative decision about it. If we do, we discuss it among ourselves and then let you know what we've decided. If we *don't*, then it's essentially forgotten."

"But why wouldn't you have decided on that?" Which was the wrong question to ask, Mary thought, because they might have pointed out the selfishness underlying her decision as their rationale for not judging it, or even as a reason for judging it negatively, though that would have been, or might have been, invalidated by the positive outcome for both parties involved: the elderly woman got all of the food she wanted and needed, and Mary was able to feel reasonably good about herself, as long as she didn't think about the guilt that her selfishness might have brought her. And as she was thinking about all of that, she realized that she'd answered her own question, and there was no reason for the judges to say anything more. And they didn't.

And then Mary laughed, which surprised her. "Well since you can see everything I do, then justice, in effect, isn't blind."

But the first judge surprised Mary by saying, "No, Mary, you're the one who's blind, because you can't see and can't understand why we're here or how we pass judgment. Unless you can but choose to ignore it. In other words, not let yourself in on what you know."

The second judge shook his head and said, "In which case Justice is the five-year-old child who covers his eyes and thinks that, because he can't see anybody, no one else can see him."

Mary shook her head, hoping to clear her mind. "And what about my concert next weekend?" she asked.

The first judge shrugged. "What about it? Your airline tickets are reserved, your motel reservation is made, posters have gone up announcing you on the campus—"

"Programs have been printed," the third judge said.

"And you're still the First Prize winner of the Graffman Competition. None of that has changed," the second judge said.

"Again," the first judge said, pressing his fingertips together, "realize how this works. Nothing, nothing at all, about your life has become any different than it ever was. The difference is in the memory of the people who knew you."

"And with that," the third judge said, "we're going to say goodbye and wish you a fair evening. Until next time, then."

And when she looked at them again they sat as still as statues on her couch, though, of course, nobody else, whether that person had known Mary or had no idea who Mary was, would have been able to see them.

The following morning, Mary wrote Ken a check for five thousand dollars. Originally she was going to make it out for ten thousand dollars, figuring that he really needed more than he'd asked for but was afraid she'd say no if he asked for too much. She didn't think she'd ever see it again, although she had no way of knowing, since she'd never given him any money before. Then she decided—a rationalization—that Ken would only get angry if she didn't send him exactly what he wanted. Or needed. To do whatever with. So after signing the check, she began to compose a letter to him, but quickly realized that, as far as he knew, she didn't exist. For a moment she considered explaining that she was a distant relative who heard he was in trouble, but how, she thought, would this "distant relative" know he needed five thousand dollars? Yes, it could be argued, if he'd asked her for it, he must have asked other people, too. But she decided not to write the letter, because all of it would sound like a fabrication once he knew her again. So she simply wrapped it in a blank sheet of white paper—Mary would always be amused when she heard someone call it "typewriter paper"—and sealed the envelope, then stamped it. It should take no more than two days to get to him, if it took that long, and although he would see that the check came from somebody who shared his last name, he would feel delighted that one relative or another was looking to help him.

Or not. Because Mary would be the first to admit that her motivation was to win herself back into the judges' good graces; she really couldn't have cared less whether Ken got out of whatever trouble he'd gotten himself into. Unless it was bad, she thought. She didn't want him standing at the receiving end of a gun. But only, of course, because she didn't want to blame herself for it. Such is the life of a family.

Four days later, the following Monday, she got an envelope in the mail with Ken's return address on it. And inside was what must have been the same sheet of white paper in which she'd wrapped her check, only this time it was enclosing that check, torn into eight pieces. At first, she had to admit, she thought and hoped it might be a letter of thanks, even as she didn't believe Ken would ever send one, but it wasn't, and what troubled her most was not the lack of appreciation on his part, but why he tore it up rather than cashed it. For a moment she wished she had someone she could talk to about it, but her friends weren't talking to her and the judges weren't available. Then she realized that she didn't need them because, given her own intuition, she could figure it out just fine. Ken was worried that the check would bounce. That it wasn't real. That he could get into trouble for cashing or depositing it. Clearly, he must have decided, someone was copying his name—*Mary* Sorabi?! Who was that?—for his or her personal gain. And then Mary felt genuinely sad that this was the kind of life her brother led. Primarily because he couldn't appreciate somebody doing something nice for him.

That night she decided to call Ellora, hoping to change Ellora's mind about Ken. She couldn't decide whether she was feeling sorry for him, genuinely loved him, or just wanted the judges to reverse their decision, but the more she thought about that last possibility, the less she believed that was what was motivating her, because she was coming to enjoy being forgotten. For one thing, she had more time to practice and more time to listen to music, and though she would ignore her telephone when it rang or one of her friends texted her, she knew that she'd have to return the call or the text eventually, and that interfered with her concentrating on what she wanted to think about. Additionally, she was tickled that Mel wouldn't bother her—yes, she decided, he was a bitter man—though she'd need to discuss things with him before her concert that weekend, and it was nice to have Ken literally disappear for a while. And then, she realized, she'd given him a reason for never calling her and never seeing her: he didn't know who she was. So she could stop fretting, as she sometimes did, over his (her?) distance. But all that said, she wanted to set things right.

So at eight o'clock that night—she hadn't listened to music first—she called Ellora. And the first thing that surprised her was that she knew Ellora's number. Why would a sister know her brother's girlfriend's telephone number? Because Ken must have been serious about her, and must have felt comfortable enough with Mary to share the information. He must have been proud. She found that surprisingly touching.

Laying comfortably on her bed, holding a full glass of tomato juice, into which she'd squeezed a lime wedge, Mary dialed Ellora's number. Ellora answered quickly. "Hello, is this Ellora?" Mary asked.

"Yes, speaking."

She sounded nervous, Mary thought, as though she knew why Mary was calling. "Ellora, my name is Miriam Fine," Mary said, using the name of her first-grade teacher, "and I'm a friend of Ken Sorabi?" She made her statement into a question because she didn't want to emphasize his name, not knowing what the relationship was like between them.

"Ken Sorabi?" Ellora asked, already sounding angry.

"Yes," Mary said. "I know you know him, and I'm a friend—"

"Look, if you're some whore that he just paid for—"

Clearly the woman was jealous, Mary thought. But why would a whore he'd just paid for be calling her?

"Ken Sorabi," Ellora said again, and laughed. "Now there's a name from my past."

Mary's heart sank. All she knew was that Ken and Ellora weren't speaking anymore; she didn't know when the break occurred.

"How do I know that you even know him?" Ellora asked.

Mary straightened herself on the bed and took a sip of juice. Well that was good, she thought. At least she didn't hang up. "I'm a friend of his from college," Mary said, wanting to emphasize that there was no liaison between her and Ken. Laughing a little, she shuddered.

"What are you drinking?" Ellora asked, but Mary couldn't decide if she sounded friendlier or more angry.

"Tomato juice," Mary said, but she almost choked.

"Right. How do I know that you're real?" Ellora asked. "What college did he go to?"

That was easy. "Syracuse University," Mary said.

That seemed to blunt some of Ellora's edginess. "Okay." A deep breath. "Where do you live?"

"Where do I *live*?" Mary asked. She thought back to Binghamton. "Johnson City," she said. "On Harry L Drive." She loved that name, thinking it was slightly surreal. Why did they name the street using someone's first name and last initial—it was his middle initial, and it was named for Harry L. Johnson, like the city—rather than his full last name?

"I see," Ellora said shrewdly. "So you're right near where he works."

And before Ellora could say "Well that explains a lot," Mary said, "We're friends from college. Just friends. And we've never been more than just friends."

At which Ellora laughed and said, "There's nothing *just* about friendship. But all right. I'll buy into your story for now."

"Thank you," Mary said.

And Ellora must have thought Mary sounded genuine, because then she said, "I'm sorry. You know, I get so many nonsense calls."

Mary nodded. "I'm sure you do." She stretched back and laid her head comfortably against her pillow, placing the glass of juice on her nightstand.

"Including calls from your friend." So Ken was still trying to reach her. That was good, because it meant that Mary might help mend whatever fissure had formed between them. But after a pause, Ellora said, "I don't want to talk to him," but quietly.

"I know that," Mary said gently. "He told me." She breathed deeply and stretched again, then lay flat on her back and looked at the ceiling. She felt like a teenager.

"So he's talking about me to other people," Ellora said, but she sounded more surprised than suspicious.

"He's talking about you to me," Mary said. "I'm his friend."

"So you say. Okay. Who are you again?"

"Miriam. Miriam Fine. I'm a friend of Ken's"—she didn't need to repeat his last name—"from school." And Mary wanted to add, "What's so hard to remember about that?" She was starting to feel unsympathetic because she really didn't want to be on the phone with Ellora. Having decided to help Ken, or help herself, she began to have her doubts, given what kind of effort it was going to take. But she also knew that if she relaxed for a moment, she would feel differently. "Look," Mary said flatly, "he's sorry for what he did."

"Sorry for what he *did*?" Ellora asked. She obviously didn't believe

Mary. "What did he do? Do you even know what he did?"

Mary told her that she didn't.

"Then what kind of friend are you?" Ellora asked.

And Mary assumed she was asking whether Mary was a good friend, who would know what had gone on between them, or a distant friend, or even an acquaintance, who would not.

But Ellora said, "No, I'm asking that literally. Seriously and literally. Are you a fuck-friend? Has he fucked you?"

Although Mary wanted to be compassionate, she was finding it difficult. Mary, who'd never been involved in a romantic relationship, so who'd never been hurt that way. But she'd been hurt in other ways, which, ultimately, were not so different, so she figured she'd let Ellora spill all of her bile, the way Ken had, and then maybe discuss things more openly and rationally once she was done. "No," she said. "That I can assure you. He's never fucked me." She was nervous but also amused. Amused by the power she'd been given. With her brother having no idea who she was, she could really screw with him. But she wasn't vindictive, and was glad not to be.

"Why not?" Ellora asked tauntingly. "Are you a dyke? Doesn't matter. He fucks them, too."

And Mary laughed, but nervously.

"What's so funny?! Look. Is this a joke? Are you really who you say you are?"

And as seriously as she could, Mary said, "I'm sorry, I'm just not used to such questions," and then she thought she sounded like she was putting on airs, like the kind of woman—too prim, too proper, too affected—that her mother used to call "an old Sally," because she had an Aunt Sally who acted like that. "All I can tell you is that Ken is a special friend to me, a *platonic* friend, and I know he's hurting because he misses you."

"All right, how much is he paying you?" Ellora asked.

Mary wanted to laugh again, but didn't. "Paying me for what?" And why did everything that had to do with Ken have to revolve around money?

"For making this phony phone call. I'm sure he's trying to set me up for something, and I'm not falling for it, so I'm sorry, sweet lady, but I've got to go."

"No! Don't!" Mary shouted, surprising herself. She sat up and took a sip of juice.

"Why not?" And Mary still couldn't figure out why Ellora hadn't hung up. Or why Ellora had even answered the phone. Mary never answered calls from strangers. Maybe Ellora was just lonely. Or maybe it was something else. "Why should I continue talking to you?" Ellora asked. "What are you going to tell me about Ken that I don't already know?"

And Mary surprised herself by saying, "The fact that he gave me your phone number."

Then, after a pause, during which, Mary thought, Ellora felt very touched, very suspicious, or didn't think about what Mary had said at all, Ellora said, "Well of course he did. He asked you to call me. He hasn't got the balls to call me himself."

"Ellora," Mary said, "I've had your phone number for the past year. He gave it to me when he started seeing you."

But then, oh damn...

"Wait a minute," Ellora said. "I know who you are."

And Mary tasted ashes in her mouth. She ran her tongue over her upper palate and lips and tried to moisten them. Had her name come up on Ellora's telephone? It shouldn't have, unless Mary had called her before, which she hadn't. But then she remembered that Ken had forgotten her, unless the judges had reversed their decision or made another decision, but no, they would have told her about that, so Ellora couldn't know she was his sister. And even if Ken had told Ellora about Mary, Ellora would have forgotten her, too.

"You're the woman who Ken dumped me for."

Mary laughed from a sense of relief, but then wondered if she herself wasn't being set up, though Mary didn't see how that would have been possible or what purpose it would have served. Then she kicked herself mentally. Does everybody do everything for a *purpose*?

"No, I'm not—" Mary said.

"Answer me one thing. How much is he paying you for this?!" Ellora was yelling. And they were back to talking about money, which made Mary wonder if Ken was paying Ellora.

"Paying me?" Mary rolled onto her left side and thought about when she could do the same thing a little while later, but to go to sleep rather than talk on the phone.

"Of course!" Ellora yelled, and Mary pulled the phone away from her ear. "He dumped you, too, and now, having run out of people to fuck over, he wants me back."

Mary could think of nothing better to say than "He's not paying me anything, because he has no money."

Ellora laughed sarcastically. "Oh, he has money. I'm sure of it. He's just not spending it on me."

And Mary began to panic. If it were true that Ken did have money, then she'd sent him the check for no reason. But no, he'd returned that. And that would mean that the judges had completely misread the situation. And why would Ken want to date a woman who was so spoiled as to complain that her boyfriend wasn't spending any or enough money on her?

"How do you know that?" Mary asked.

"I don't know," Ellora said, still angry, "I just know." And then she surprised Mary by laughing. "I don't know *how* I know, I just know *that* I know."

"I've seen his house," Mary said. "He doesn't spend his money on that."

"No," Ellora said, "he certainly doesn't. I live better than he does."

"And he makes a good living, but—," Mary said, and was going to tell Ellora that maybe it wasn't as good a living as they'd both assumed, but Ellora interrupted her.

"I'm sure he does," Ellora said, "but—"

"But what?" Mary asked. And realized that Ellora didn't sound angry anymore.

"If he doesn't spend any of it on me, he must—"

"Yes?" Mary asked.

"He must be spending it on someone else."

Mary shook her head. "If it's even there. Ellora, look. If he has it, and I'm not saying that he does or he doesn't, because I don't know. But if he does, he's not spending it on someone else."

"How do you know that?" Ellora asked.

"Because he talks only about you."

"Why should I believe you?" Ellora asked.

And Mary smiled. "Because you want to," she said. "And that's the only reason any of us believe whatever we think is true." She shook her head slowly. She didn't realize how much she was learning from the judges.

"Look, Miriam," Ellora said, "you're a sweet woman. I can tell that by talking to you. A sweet woman and a good friend, and Ken is lucky to have someone like you in his life."

And where did *that* come from?, Mary wondered. It was funny how people could let their anger build to a pitch so slowly but then let it all go in an instant.

"But—," Ellora said.

"*But?*" Mary asked. She sat up and scratched the back of her neck.

"I don't know if I want to go back. Yet."

Mary was relieved, because she could feel the conversation winding down and maybe accomplishing what she'd wanted it to. She looked at her glass of tomato juice. There would be plenty left to enjoy when the conversation was over.

"So it was your decision," Mary said. "Because that's what Ken—"

"Yes," Ellora said, still quiet and almost contrite. "It was my decision. But tell him—"

"Yes?" Mary asked.

"Tell the fucker...." And she stopped. "Tell him I said hello," Ellora said, then added, "I don't care anymore," but she was speaking away from the phone, which meant she did care.

"Ellora, I want to ask you just one more question."

A deep breath. "Sure."

"Did he ever hurt you?"

"Hurt me?!" For a moment Mary thought she sounded angry again, but then realized that Ellora was just surprised. "Of course," Ellora said. "When?"

And Ellora said, "The last time he said goodbye." And that must have hurt Ellora more than she realized it would, because a moment later she hung up without saying goodbye.

Still, Mary understood, or thought she understood. Ellora had ended her relationship with Ken because she was suspicious, and although she wanted to continue seeing him, her fear of being pushed aside overwhelmed whatever pleasure the relationship might have brought. Mary thought about a story Julietta had once told her, Leila, and Lizzy. An elderly woman living in the East Village was thrown into a state of crippling panic when she heard that a man was murdering other women of her age in her neighborhood. So the woman decided to swallow poison and kill herself. Mary knew that a lot of people who took their own lives thought of suicide as the ultimate act of control. And Ellora was looking to take charge of her situation but decided she didn't like the way control felt. Which was sad, Mary thought. Because things might get better.

When Mary lay the phone facedown on her nightstand, she finished her glass of tomato juice. Her question about Ken hurting Ellora would go unanswered. What Mary had really wanted to know was whether Ken ever hit her—he'd never hit Mary—or insulted her or made any prejudiced statements toward her, but Mary was sure that he hadn't, because she was Indian, just like Ken. Ken, who wanted to forget, seemingly, that half of his family was Chinese. But explaining any of that to Ellora would have meant more time on the phone, and she didn't want to plant any ideas in Ellora's mind that Ken could be belligerent, if she didn't know that already.

And she wouldn't find out where Ken's money was going, if he even had any, but likely Ellora knew no more than Mary did. And that, at least, bonded them; their assumption about Ken's finances, which may have been wrong. Though that would mean that the judges knew what they were talking about, and that, as it always did, relaxed Mary. For a moment she worried that Ellora would tell Ken what happened, if and when they started talking again, and Ken would swear that he'd never heard of a Miriam

Fine, but no, Mary realized, that would only make Ellora suspicious, and that was something Ken wouldn't want to do, and Ken would never deny being known by someone, even if he had no idea who it was.

So, in the end, she fell asleep early and slept well, thinking only about her flight to Iowa that Friday, and repeating her winning program the next night, at a small college she'd never heard of, in a small town she'd never heard of, and wondering if, by that time, anybody would have heard of her.

IV

J inete College was a small liberal arts school with fewer than five thousand undergraduate students. Its campus occupied three hundred eight-seven acres in the northwest corner of Yagoda, Iowa, which was thirty-nine miles northeast of Cedar Rapids, and whose population was slightly less than that of the school. It was a picturesque little village, with a broad boulevard, South Rapids Road and North Rapids Road, intersected by its main thoroughfare, Eberle Street. Downtown was a street corner, but there one could find, radiating from it for a block in each direction, a furniture gallery, a carpeting and interiors store, a Chinese restaurant called the Green Dragon, a Protestant church, a luncheonette, a men's and women's clothing store, a bank, an optometrist's office, a pawn shop, a sporting goods store, and a tattoo parlor. Cutting diagonally between North Rapids Road and Eberle Street was Lera Street, which ran for five blocks. On one side was the college campus, and on the other side was the president's house, several blocks of ranch houses, and a small art museum.

Although she'd never been to Iowa, Mary grew up with a vaguely positive impression of it. She remembered her mother telling her how, when she was in the fourth grade in the New York City public school system, her class had to take "the Iowa test," which was a national IQ test—not so named—in which students were asked hundreds of questions in a neatly printed booklet, that they could answer on a separate sheet of paper by marking a series of lettered ellipses with their sharpened number 2 pencils. Iowa, Mary had been told, had, or once had, the highest number of literate residents in America. It was also where Dvořák lived during the summer of 1893, and where he wrote his *New World Symphony*, among other works.

INTERVIEWER: Are there any places you really don't want to perform in?

MARY: Las Vegas. The city with a museum devoted to Liberace and nine out of ten people who've never heard of Mendelssohn.

INTERVIEWER: Don't be an elitist.

MARY: I'm not being an elitist at all, but I'm not surprised you didn't pick up on that. And make it ninety-nine out of a hundred, to be more accurate. Here's the problem. Classical music is a specialized art form, but it's sold in the entirely wrong way. It's geared to appeal to a real minority of people, people who pride themselves on being in a minority, and if more people, even if, God forbid, the masses, started to find it attractive, it would lose its allure. It would become common.

INTERVIEWER: Okay, understood.

MARY: You know how I developed my love of classical music? From my father. You know how he developed his love of it? Through watching Saturday morning cartoons. Racist fare, yes, often, but at least they brought culture to children.

INTERVIEWER: Nobly.

MARY (*Laughs*): Oh, please, there was nothing noble about it. The producers used it because it was in the public domain, so it saved them the cost of hiring people to write background music. Classical music, when my father was growing up, was also taught in the schools, in "music appreciation" classes. Now? No. So don't tell me I'm being an elitist. (*Laughs*) And as for Las Vegas, well, it's like the Midwest. Wide-open spaces don't appeal to me.

The days leading up to her trip found Mary surprisingly happy. Mary didn't like surprises, and though happiness was always nice, this was a happiness she wasn't used to. The lack of familiarity that other people had with her allowed her to feel unencumbered, more relaxed, but also more in control. And if she didn't embrace that happiness as tightly as she might have, she knew that soon things would return to normal and she would be remembered again, so the happiness wouldn't last. With that in mind, she wondered if she really wanted to go back to the way things were. Maybe starting over fresh was what she preferred. But if that were even an option, why had the judges made this her penalty? Unless it wasn't a penalty at all, just a different way of living. Though for someone who desired constancy as much as Mary did, difference could always be considered a penalty.

The day after she spoke to Ellora, she drove to her bank to withdraw enough money for her trip. The teller was discrete and polite, but when she asked him if he remembered her—to see if anything had changed—he shook his head and explained that he was new.

Then on Wednesday, Mel called, as she knew he would. She didn't always enjoy talking to him on the phone. When he called, he had an agenda he wanted to get through before asking her if she had anything to say, and he hated being interrupted, and when she called, he made it seem like she was imposing on his time. At least that was how she felt during their conversations, but afterward she could shrug it off and let herself know that he *was* busy. As though she weren't. She would always tell herself that Mel was the perfect name for him, because it started with "Me."

And yet, talking to him on the phone was better than seeing him face to face. When she'd first met him, three years earlier, she'd been escorted into his office, something she'd found unusually formal, being more used to people walking out and greeting her. He was short but so thin as to appear malnourished. To Mary he looked like a six-year-old child with a sixty-year-old man's face. His skin was olive and slightly oily, his dark brown hair was slicked back and parted not quite in the middle but not quite on the side, which Mary found surprisingly unsettling, and his heavy, droopy eyelids, which reminded Mary of canvas, covered eyes that were red on the bottom. His eyebrows were bushy, and his piscine lips looked as though they were about to slide off his face. But once he started talking she gawked at him, and though she couldn't have been the first person to do so, she felt terrible for staring. That was when he said, "Don't ask, and I'll tell." In later years she would be fond of recounting that story by embellishing it with his having said, "But if you do ask, I'll never forgive you." Which, of course, he hadn't said and never would.

"Seven years ago I suffered a minor stroke that left the left...no, I'm not stuttering...side of my face frozen. Okay, paralyzed, but I'd rather say 'frozen.' Not that there's going to be a thaw anytime soon. Though there might be. Maybe."

And she hadn't known what to say, except—and God knows what possessed her—"Maybe you ought to be a pianist, then, like me. Because the audience is only going to see the right side of your face."

And he smacked his open right palm down on his bulky walnut desk, and that scared her, before he laughed for too long and too loudly and said, "Until I turn to acknowledge the applause." Then he shrugged and said quietly, "Well, it prevents me from talking out of both sides of my mouth." But the voice was too harsh to imply friendliness or, at least, an appreciation of her humor. "But I don't smile," he said. "Not because I'm unhappy, but because I can't." Which left open the question of whether he was unhappy. "You see, the left side of my lips won't move, so when I turn the right side up it looks like a smirk. But I'm a behind-the-scenes man, so who cares?"

She figured that she must have felt immediately comfortable with him to say what she'd said, and then for him to say as much as he'd said, but comfort was never to follow, and their relationship remained cool. Mary would always think that was his decision—keeping people at a "safe" distance because he was "handicapped"—and it would never occur to her that she kept equally as much distance from most people. But why should it? To Mary, keeping a distance was so familiar that she never thought about it. Especially with Mel, the man she often saw as a harlequin, one side being the opposite of the other.

"Hello, Ms....Sorabi," Mel said. "I'd like to introduce myself. I'm Mel Stargell, and I'm an agent. A musician's agent. And my boss, Bertie Seipel, asked me to call you because I understand you're giving a recital at the Jinete College on Saturday night this week."

It was ten o'clock in the morning. Mary was sitting at her kitchen table, having just finished breakfast—a glass of orange juice and a poached egg on toast—and was slowly sipping her second cup of black coffee. Mary thought Mel sounded like he was reading from a script, but the lack of opening up the conversation to her was entirely typical.

"Ms. S.," he said, and Mary hated that. He'd called her Ms. S. the first time they'd met, and even after she'd asked him not to, he'd continued it for at least a month into their professional relationship.

"Please call me Mary," she said.

"Whatever you say, Ms. S. Anyway, I'm calling because I have an issue with the program you're planning to perform."

"*You* have an issue or *Bertie* has an issue?"

"Bertie?" Mel asked. "You know him?"

"Of course I know him," Mary said. "I met him once before."

"Whatever. Anyway, Ms. S., Mr. Seipel and I have an issue with your program, and I'd like to discuss it with you if that's all right."

Mary looked down and thought what a good idea it would be to count the number of tiles on her kitchen floor. "Yeah, sure," she said.

"Okay. Change it."

"Change it?" Mary asked, and shut her eyes.

"Did I not make myself clear?" Mel asked. "Change it. Please."

Mel was never overtly nasty or hostile or even disrespectful, but he believed that whatever he told anyone should be followed exactly, and when people questioned him, as he thought Mary was doing, he got irritated. But the fact that he never yelled and never lost his temper, which would have been wholly unprofessional, actually unnerved Mary more, because the possibility of an explosion was often more threatening than an explosion itself.

Mary looked around her. "Why?" The sunlight was streaming through the kitchen windows, letting her see the shore, where there were already small clusters of people and umbrellas being planted and raised. She felt relaxed. Relaxed because nobody, including Mel, knew her anymore, relaxed because she wasn't outside, particularly not on the shore with the other people, who still, Mary thought, seemed to be enjoying themselves, and relaxed thinking about her flight to Iowa two days later. Visit Yagoda, Iowa. One more thing to scratch off her bucket list.

"Why?" Mel asked. Mary hated it when people repeated her questions, though she did the same thing. "Because I said so?" And after Mary didn't say anything, Mel laughed. "No, seriously, because a program like that won't fly in Yagoda, Iowa. People there don't like contemporary music."

"Mel," Mary said. She sighed. "May I call you Mel?"

"Of course."

"*Mel*, Schoenberg wrote his Suite almost a hundred years ago. How much longer are people going to think the twentieth century is contemporary?"

And after a pause, he said, "Look, I'm not going to argue with you," though his delivery was clipped. "I'm just passing along what Bertie said."

Of course. Always pin a losing argument on someone else. And he knew he was losing.

"If you want to cancel my appearance, cancel my appearance," Mary said.

"No!" he shouted. "I'm not saying that. You're famous now. Relatively."

Mary sipped her coffee. So Mel at least knew who she was, from her win almost three weeks earlier, but didn't remember her. "Isn't fame always relative?" she asked. Her coffee was starting to get cold and bitter.

"Okay, look at it like this," Mel said. "Your program *might*, and I want to emphasize 'might,' go over with a sophisticated Philadelphia audience. Remember, nobody less than Leopold Stokowski used to lead the Philadelphia Orchestra and gave it their sound. And he championed contemporary music. But it won't fly in Yagoda, Iowa."

Mary understood that one hires an "expert" in anything so one doesn't have to think. It's not just working, it's thinking. If she needed drywall repair, she would call an expert so she wouldn't have to think about what needs to be done or how it's done, only how much it's going to cost. And the same should have been true of an agent. He would find venues for her to perform in, so she wouldn't have to exert any effort, mental or physical, in finding one or making the appropriate arrangements. But one thing about hiring an expert is that you had to trust him, which is to say, you had to believe he knew what he was doing. If Mel really thought that her program of Prokofiev, Schoenberg, and Ravel would go over the heads of a group of people, mostly college students, in Middle America, which was just like America anywhere else, except that it was moved to the plains, he clearly didn't have a feel for what audiences thought. Or so she believed. And yet, she stuck with him, and, to support her decision, *believed* him, sometimes, because she was so reluctant to change. But that time she thought he was wrong. She'd play her program, which, she knew, was in no way "difficult" to comprehend.

"I'm sorry, Mel. I understand and respect your position, but programs have already been printed, posters have already gone up, I'm thinking, and people have bought tickets knowing what I'm going to play. It went over well with—"

"An audience of judges," he said. "They're specialists. You're not playing for specialists now."

Mary was genuinely offended and insulted. Not just for herself but for the people who would be attending her recital. She really believed that they wanted to hear the music she was going to perform. But that, of course, was because she *had* to believe it. If she didn't, what would she have left? So much of being a performing artist, she thought, dealt with illusion. Somebody big, somebody famous, somebody special walks onto the stage and the audience, after a moment or two, quiets down and starts to applaud, because they know they're going to be entertained, and possibly captivated. But maybe that wasn't it at all. Maybe they were applauding because the artist was giving them something to do. Their poker game, or their pinochle game, or their bridge game got cancelled. The movie they were hoping to see wasn't playing in their local cinema anymore. Their friends, whom they were going to visit, suddenly got sick or forgotten they'd made "other plans." Or maybe there was nothing worth watching on television that night—Mary didn't know; she didn't own a TV. So without anything better to do, they decided they would give a concert of classical music a try. Maybe, Mary thought, that was what really got audiences out. Though for once, she decided, she wouldn't mind being wrong.

"So what I'd like you to do," Mel said. "Hello? Are you still there?"

"I'm still here," Mary said, kicking off her slippers and running her right foot along the smooth tiles of her kitchen floor.

"Okay," Mel said anxiously. "Look, I have another call coming in, so I'm going to have to make this quick, but what I think you should do is get out on stage and announce that you're going to change the program. Trust me, Ms. S. Nobody these days has the patience for Schoenberg."

"Mel," she said, "the Suite lasts fifteen minutes."

INTERVIEWER: Do you think people have a shorter attention span now, with all the—

MARY (*Interrupts him*): All the what? Other things competing for their attention? Of course not. It's always been that way. A long attention span isn't part of human nature. Look at the slow movement of Haydn's *Surprise Symphony*. He interjected a loud chord after... what? Fifteen bars of slow, quiet music, because he knew his audience was already nodding off. And that was more than two hundred years ago.

INTERVIEWER: Then how do you explain Wagner, whose music dramas can last four or five hours?

MARY: Wagner, I think, was unique, because he either had or *thought* he had people who were so enamored of everything he wrote that he could compose five hours of relatively uninterrupted music—remember, there were no breaks for arias or ensembles, it was just a continuous wash of sound for, as you said, four or five hours—with a clear conscience.

"I'm sorry, Ms. S.," Mel said. "I'm going to have to call you back. Is this the best number to reach you?"

Mary yawned, deliberately loudly. "It is."

"And how late can I call?"

"Call whenever you want," Mary said, and after he said thank you and hung up, Mary thought, You're just going to be talking to yourself.

That afternoon Mary practiced the three pieces she was planning to play that Saturday night: the Prokofiev Piano Sonata No. 8 in B-Flat Major, Op.

84, Schoenberg's Suite for Piano, Op. 25, and Ravel's *Gaspard de la nuit*, but she also practiced the Brahms *Variations and Fugue on a Theme by Handel*, Op. 24, both because she'd been getting it into her fingers lately, as she would have told anyone who'd cared to ask, and because she wondered whether she should replace at least one of the contemporary works with it. She wasn't about to blame Mel for anything—she wouldn't give him that privilege—but she did end up questioning how anxiously her audience wanted to hear the kind of music—and she loathed that expression, because it marginalized what it was referring to—that she loved.

And for a while she started to wonder, and not for the first time, whether she liked the "right" things. And "right" was always a dangerous label to apply. There was nothing wrong with liking things that most people didn't. She'd even explained that to the interviewer, and then wondered what, if he had printed his article, her interview might have sounded like. Perhaps she would have come across as an idiot. Or completely self-absorbed.

INTERVIEWER: Do you like Elliott Carter's music?

MARY: Very much. Especially the chamber music, the songs, and the concertos. In that order. That's where I think he was at his best.

INTERVIEWER: What about his piano music?

MARY: He didn't write very much of it, but what he did write is good, just not in the same league as the other categories I mentioned.

INTERVIEWER: A lot of people find his music intellectual and dry.

MARY (*Laughs*): What does that mean? What are they listening to? What are they hearing?

INTERVIEWER: I—

MARY (*Interrupts*): How can you find a collection of notes "intellectual"? I think they're reading too much into it. Do they mean it's super-intelligently put together? I have no doubt that it is, but so is a lot of great music. You understand, of course, that I'm just speaking rhetorically, right?

INTERVIEWER: I—

MARY (*Interrupts*): I think what people mean is that they don't understand it, as though music needs to be understood to be appreciated.

It doesn't. But they find it intimidating so they attribute to it some quality they can't grasp. "It's beyond my realm of comprehension. I'm not smart enough to understand it." That's what they're saying, but that's so sad. I have no idea how Niagara Falls was formed but I still find it beautiful.

INTERVIEWER: Okay, understood, but Carter's music isn't seductive.

MARY: Says who? Look, people thrive on stimulation. If they can't be stimulated sexually they look to be stimulated emotionally, and if they can't be stimulated emotionally they look to be stimulated intellectually. And some people *hate* Carter's music, but that's good. Hatred is stimulating. I'd rather hate a piece of music than be bored by it, because if I hate it I'll come back to it to find out why, whereas if I'm bored I'll just walk away. (*Pauses*) What can I tell you? I guess I'm just different.

INTERVIEWER (*Apologetically*): Don't say that. Maybe you're not as different as you think you are.

And that really angered Mary, because that was something she hated; being thought of as *not* different. All her life she knew she was different. She was of two ethnicities, neither of which was like that of most of the people around her. She loved classical music. She loved twentieth-century classical music. She desired solitude. And after hating herself for those things for years, she learned to accept them, then love them, and finally be proud of them. So to be thought of as being like everyone else scared her, not because she didn't like other people—she did, in her way—but because she thought most other people were unhappy, and she didn't want to think of herself that way. Anymore.

"Maybe you're not as happy as you think you are," Julietta had once told her, angrily. The semper-melancholy Julietta always reminded Mary of her mother. And that comment bothered her, too, though, ultimately, it was nonsensical because, by definition, we are however we feel we are. Perhaps that point was lost on Julietta.

Mel called her back at ten o'clock that night. She was laying in bed, reading. If she'd been listening to music she wouldn't have answered her phone, and called him back the next day, but a book was easier to put aside. Happily, it was *The Collected Short Stories of Saki*, and many of them were only two or three pages long, so she managed to just finish the one she was involved in before the ringing stopped.

"Yes, Mel."

"Ms. S.," Mel said slowly and, Mary thought, a little sadly. Was something wrong? "I'm sorry. Mary. How are you?"

Mary exhaled loudly. "About the same as I was the last time I spoke to you, only more tired."

"Then I won't make this long," he said, and Mary felt optimistic. "Change your program."

"Mel, we had this conversation before. I'm not going to change it," she said. And then, after Mel didn't say anything in return, she tried a new tack. "Change it to what?"

Mel laughed. "I don't know," he said. "I was just assigned to you. I don't know what's in your repertoire. Play some Beethoven; everybody likes him. Play all Beethoven. A concert of three sonatas would be nice. But make them long ones. Can you do that?"

"No, Mel, I can't, because Beethoven isn't in my repertoire; twentieth-century music is. And...I hate to tell you this, but not everybody likes him."

INTERVIEWER: What do you think of Beethoven?

MARY: I don't know, I've never met him.

INTERVIEWER: You know what I mean.

MARY: I don't like his music at all.

INTERVIEWER: Why not?

MARY: Because, to me, it lacks the one thing I prize most in music. Vulnerability. I hear none of it in any of his works. Well, maybe occasionally, but not much. To me he tries too hard, especially in his so-called middle-period works, which are the pieces most people are familiar with. Always trying to say something big, loud, uplifting, inspiring, transcendent. It's hectoring.

INTERVIEWER: He's said to have suffered a lot. That should make his music sound vulnerable.

MARY: You would think so, wouldn't you? And that brings up another point. To me, and again, this is only how I hear it and how I feel about it, he sounds like somebody who was so afraid of revealing his inner feelings that his music takes on an air of artificiality. And I find that very off-putting. You know, when I listen to him I want to shout back, "I'd believe you if you'd just stop yelling."

INTERVIEWER: You can't say all of his music is loud.

MARY: I'm not, and it isn't. A lot of his late pieces are very inward. And they, at least, are far more interesting to me than his earlier works, but they still don't move me. It's as though, in his last works, he's contemplating his life from a distance, but never letting himself in.

INTERVIEWER (*Excitedly*): Then you see?! That's exactly what I was saying before. You find Beethoven's music "intellectualized," and that's the problem people have with Elliott Carter and his ilk.

MARY: I didn't know Carter had an ilk, but at least his music is interesting, and much more emotive, to me, than Beethoven's.

"Is twentieth-century music all you perform?" Mel asked.

Mary was surprised to realize how annoying it could be to not have someone remember her. Well, it was fine if the person didn't talk. "No, but that constitutes the majority of it."

"Then try some Debussy, just nothing too outré."

Mary rolled her eyes. She could imagine Mel patting himself on the back for using a French word in a statement about Debussy. "Mel, let me decide when I get there."

"And that's what I wanted to talk to you about," Mel said. "Your getting there. And being there."

Mary loved sleeping under a down comforter. Anything less made her feel naked and exposed. It was fine, of course, for keeping her warm in the winter, when she would set the heat low, but in the summer she had to turn down the thermostat to sixty degrees so she could sleep comfortably. Snuggling beneath the comforter that night, she listened to Mel go over the details of her flight, her motel reservation, and how she would get from one place to the other. Without that comforter, she thought, she would have fallen asleep two sentences into their conversation.

"Now let me tell you about Steve Manillo," he said.

"Steve Manillo?" She repeated the name to make sure she'd heard it correctly.

"Yes," Mel said. "And that's Ma-*nill*-o, not like *Man*-i-low, though you're probably too young to remember who Barry Manilow was."

And Mary thought, Oh, for the days of the old rotary phone, when you could just slam down the receiver.

"Anyway, he's going to be your contact person, your go-to man in Iowa. You'll meet him at the motel on Saturday morning. I'll send you a picture of him so you know what he looks like, and his number. He already has yours."

And Mel gave her the necessary information about her flight, her motel reservation, and what she could expect to find when she got to the college.

"What do people do out there?" Mary asked.

"Sit by their kitchen windows and watch tornedos for fun," he said. "As long as they stay in the distance."

"The people or the tornados?" she asked.

"Both," he said.

She smiled, not because she thought Mel was clever—Mary never thought Mel was clever—but because she had cousins living in Champaign, Illinois and remembered thinking, the first time she visited them, how far the horizon stretched, so not just how far away everything seemed but how much larger the world looked. She was used to looking at the ocean from her living room windows, but the flat, open lands seemed much more vast and, ultimately, more humbling.

"And you've got the Bryden Perrett Art Museum on the campus,"—it wasn't on the campus, it was across the street—"and who knows? Maybe you'll be lucky and they'll have an exhibit of handmade quilts or something."

She rolled her eyes again and thought about the glasses she wore at her recitals. If the light him them in just the right way, nobody could see her eyes rolling. Then she thought about Mel and wondered if it wasn't a disadvantage that he didn't know her, at least for then. Because he was trying harder to impress her with his corniness, what he liked to think of as his folkish humor—which should have been foreign to a man who grew up in New York—and she would be better off when he remembered her once more.

On Friday, Mary boarded her flight for Cedar Rapids at Philadelphia International Airport just after nine o'clock in the morning. The flight would take four hours, including a one-hour layover in Chicago. Having to stop for an hour on a trip that would have taken three hours had the flight been direct made Mary feel that she was limping to Iowa rather than flying. She would land by one o'clock that afternoon, then be driven to her motel, where she would check in and relax.

Driving into Philadelphia again, for the first time since her win three weeks earlier, Mary felt more excited than she expected to. In fact, she felt important. And yet, when she boarded the plane, looked around her, and saw that nobody recognized her, or seemed to recognize her, she felt a little disappointed. Well, maybe not disappointed; perhaps sobered would be a better word. But then she thought how silly it was to expect people to point their fingers at her and say, "Hey! I know you!" Or whatever it was people did when they casually saw somebody famous. She'd never seen anyone under those circumstances, and she'd never been famous, so she didn't know.

Her accommodation was at the Tellory Inn in Jorgensen, which was fifteen miles south of Yagoda, so farther from the airport, and half an hour from the college. Surely Mel could have found her something closer. But maybe not. She was greeted at East Iowa Airport by a rotund man in middle age, with graying hair, a full mustache and beard, and sunglasses. Although Mary wore glasses whenever she performed, she was suspicious of people who wore sunglasses. Not being able to see someone's eyes prevented her from understanding a lot of what that person was trying to express. Or, more accurately, was expressing without trying. But he smiled and Mary felt comfortable with him, especially as he didn't say anything except "Hello" and "Thank you" during the hour-long drive to the motel. She never learned his name.

The lobby, like most motel lobbies, looked like a well-appointed living room with too much furniture. She looked at the table lamps and wondered why they were needed, as there were pot lights in the ceiling, but then reminded herself that they were there to suggest hominess. But to her they suggested artificiality, something accented by the noise and sheer number of strangers around her. And in the end all she could think of was sitting in a funeral parlor, whose similar evocation of hominess struck her as equally phony. She also marveled over how many shades of beige there were.

Walking into her room and seeing that the wallpaper was almost the same color as the walls in her living room, Mary felt sad that she never quite appreciated leaving her house. Many people loved getting away from their familiar surroundings and being someplace different, but Mary's familiar surroundings were so satisfying that getting away from them held no attraction. A hotel or a motel was just someplace to wait—a waiting room—until she could get out on stage, do what she loved, and leave.

Her first thought was to relax, but she hated relaxing. She needed to be stimulated; relaxation depressed her. She had her book of Saki short stories with her, but wasn't comfortable enough yet to lay down and read any. She couldn't call her friends—not that she would have—so she opened her laptop and looked at the website for Jinete College. She'd avoided doing that before her trip, because she was afraid to discover something that would disappoint her, though she couldn't imagine what that could be, as she really hadn't thought about the college at all. But she was able to locate the Sylvan Hodge Student Center, where she would ask whoever drove her there to drop her off, as that was the building nearest the campus' main entrance, and the Rosalind Elliott Theater, where she would be performing the following night.

Then she closed her laptop and looked outside. The flat openness around her seemed to inspire quiet, or perhaps quietness just fit the surroundings. Looking out her window, she got a feeling of solitude that wasn't altogether to her liking. A sort of enforced solitude rather than a desired solitude. Desolation. There was a difference between solitude and desolation just as there was a difference between nostalgia and sadness. It must have been the absence of anything to focus on. So she slept that afternoon, had dinner, which she found unremarkable, in the motel's restaurant, and then walked back to her room to read. As soon as she got there she felt better, because the room was already starting to feel familiar, but that feeling faded a few minutes later, so after reading she went to sleep. It wasn't even eight o'clock.

When she awoke the next morning, the first thing Mary told herself was, Today is the big day. In a way it felt like a bigger day than the day of the competition, because she'd never entered a competition before, so she had no idea how it was going to feel. But she'd given many recitals, and knew at least some of what would follow, though as this was her first recital since winning the competition, she felt added pressure to not disappoint anyone who might have heard her in Philadelphia. Of course, she couldn't imagine that anyone who'd been there would have flown out to Iowa, but she was trying to think of herself as a celebrity, before deciding that that wasn't who she was, and wasn't who she wanted to be. So, as always, she decided she'd just try to please herself.

She showered, dressed, and ate breakfast in the hotel's restaurant. She enjoyed it—a glass of tomato juice, pancakes with "fresh" strawberries that tasted thawed, whipped cream, and "real" maple syrup that came out of a bottle—more than she'd enjoyed her dinner, but she was too anxious to have coffee, so she drank two cups of green tea.

Mel had mentioned an art museum on the grounds of the campus, but, as Mary had found out from the college's website, it was across the street. She would spend an hour there, she thought, then get to the theater. She hoped someone would let her try out the piano she was going to play that night, but wasn't sure. Sometimes she could practice on a strange instrument, sometimes not. But that was what Steve Manillo was for, so she decided to call him. The only problem, she then realized, was that Mel never sent her Steve's number or picture, so she had no way to get in touch with him. Why? Had Mel already forgotten her, or forgotten her again, after he got off the phone with her the second time? That wouldn't have made sense, because he'd remembered her when they spoke that Wednesday night, and the judges hadn't told her that she'd be repeatedly forgotten, only forgotten by anybody who'd known her. Which still left her open, as it were, to rediscovery. Forgetting her again would be cruel, and the judges, she was sure, weren't cruel.

Then she wondered why she hadn't thought about Steve's number before. But that was because she really didn't want it, as she believed she really didn't need it. She could handle things on her own. Unless Steve was the only person that any of the people at the college would be expecting or willing to speak with about her recital that night.

So, sitting in the lobby, she called Mel, but got a busy signal, and that surprised her. She'd never heard a busy signal on a cell phone. So she tried again but got the same signal. She couldn't even leave a message. So she texted him, explaining who she was, and that she needed—not wanted—Steve Manillo's number. She waited half an hour, and when she didn't hear back, she looked at the people sitting around her, but as she had no idea what Steve looked like, she didn't know if he was there or not, and she didn't know whether he would recognize her. Likely he would, she told herself, but then wondered if she was just building herself up.

When nobody approached her, she walked to the front desk. Then she felt more relaxed, maybe because she was doing something. She was greeted by the man who'd checked her in the day before. His name was Ernie, as she'd learned from his name tag, and Mary always loved that name, because it was her maternal grandfather's name, and he was a jovial, loquacious, and articulate man, like her father. A male friend of Mary's once told her that all women marry their fathers, but Mary figured that only a man would say that. This Ernie, however—tall, slender, and young, with short, dark brown hair combed straight down on his forehead, and pale, flat lips that had yet to break into a smile—reminded her nothing of her grandfather.

"Excuse me," she said quietly.

"Yes?" Ernie said loudly, implying that she needed to speak up.

"I'm looking for Steve Manillo."

Ernie was staring at his computer screen and shook his head without looking at her. "Nobody by that name works here."

Embarrassed, Mary laughed. "No," she said. "He's a guest. At least I think he's a guest."

"Do you know when he checked in?" Ernie asked.

"Probably today," Mary said.

Ernie looked at her and nodded. His demeanor softened. "Give me a minute, please, and I'll check." Ernie must have had something pressing on his mind, Mary thought. He couldn't have been bothered by her question. But Ernie shook his head again and said, very sympathetically, "I'm sorry, but there's nobody here by that name."

"Can you page him?" Mary asked.

"Page him? Give me a moment, please," Ernie said, though he looked annoyed.

Sitting down on a couch that faced away from the front desk—Mary didn't want to see how Ernie would occupy his time before getting on the PA system—Mary thought about how much she hated waiting for anyone or anything. It made her feel vulnerable. She could be having a perfectly marvelous morning, but if she knew someone was coming to visit, work, or even drop off a package, she would forget all about whatever was making her happy and concentrate on the waiting. Not the guest, the waiting. Waiting for the sake of waiting.

After a few minutes, during which Mary didn't hear Steve's name paged, she walked back to the front desk, but Ernie was gone. In his place was a taller, more heavily set, older man with a pencil-thin black mustache and puffy lips. He smiled. "Yesssssssssss," he said. The word seemed to slither.

"Could you page Steve Manillo for me, please? He's either a guest or a visitor here, and I need to speak with him." She was anxious.

The man closed his eyes, nodded curtly, and said, "Of course." Then, "Steve Manillo. Steve Manillo. Will you please come to the front desk? You have a guest waiting to speak with you."

Mary liked that, and she felt better than she had all morning. But no one came forward. And without Mary having to say anything, the receptionist repeated his announcement, a shade louder, and by then, Mary was sure, everyone in the lobby was looking at her, so she stared off into space, letting her vision blur.

"I'm sorry," the receptionist said, "he doesn't seem to be here."

But he sounded so friendly, unlike Ernie, that Mary then wished Ernie were back. He, at least, seemed more authentic. Pure. The new receptionist was just putting on a show. No wonder nobody responded to the page.

Rather than walk back to her room, Mary sat in a chair that faced the front entrance, in case Steve came walking in, and just as she did that, he called. The number that showed up on her phone was unfamiliar, but she knew it was him.

"Hello?"

"Mary!"

"Yes. This is Mary. Steve?"

"Of course!" The voice was pleasant if a touch nasal.

"I'm so glad you called, because Mel never sent me—"

And Steve laughed, then clicked his tongue. "Mel. Forget about Mel for now. *I'm* here."

"Where?" She stood up.

"Oh, right," Steve said, sounding fuddled. "I'm at the college."

Mary wanted to be angry because that was not the way things were supposed to happen, and she hated it when her plans got derailed, even if she hadn't made them herself. But she was too glad to hear from Steve to feel any animosity. "I thought you were supposed to meet me here, at my motel. In fact, Mel told me that you'd be checking in today. This morning." She looked at her watch. It was only eleven o'clock.

"Um, what motel are you in?"

"The Tellory Inn in Jorgensen."

Another click of the tongue. "Jesus Christ, what did he book you there for? You're half an hour from the campus. All right, tell you what. Grab a lift over here, go to the Student Center; it's called the Sylvan Hodge Student Center"—Mary knew—"and ask for me."

"I'm on my way," Mary said.

When she got back to the front desk, Ernie was standing behind it. He looked at her but didn't say anything.

"I need a ride to Jinete College," she said.

"Right," Ernie said flatly. "I'll call somebody from Four Kings."

"Who are they?" Mary asked.

"They're our local car service."

"I've never heard of them," Mary said.

"Of course you haven't," Ernie said, holding the telephone but not changing the expression on his face. "They're local."

Did she hear him laugh?

"But they all drive light gray Honda Civics. Don't ask me why," he said. "I guess it makes them easier to recognize."

And it's cheaper than painting your name on the car, Mary thought. She felt disappointed for a moment, but attributed that to anxiety over that night's concert. She walked into the vestibule in front of the lobby a few minutes later, and waited, but as soon as the sliding glass doors slid open—she was standing on the entry mat—she saw a light gray Honda Civic pull up. She walked outside, and the driver lowered his front passenger window. "Mary?" he asked, leaning toward it.

"Yes," she said, and laughed. She didn't know why; possibly she was relieved at not having to wait. And kudos, she thought, to the car service for getting someone there so quickly.

"Jinete College, right?" the driver asked.

"That's it," Mary said.

"Come on in!"

She liked his appearance. He was young, had medium-length dirty blond hair, parted on the right, and a round but not heavy face, slightly flat. His eyes were narrow and pale blue, his nose sharp, and he wore a pair of gold wireframe glasses whose lenses looked exceptionally clean; good for a driver. He also had a neatly trimmed mustache and beard that looked just a shade redder than his hair. His smile was placid. For reasons that Mary couldn't fathom, he reminded her of Jesse, though he looked nothing like him, and Mary thought about how people always see others in terms of people they know, never in terms of the people themselves. It's the rare person who reminds us of no one, and would we even want to meet someone like that?

Turning around from the front seat he extended his right hand to Mary, who was sitting on the passenger side in the back. "Wilbur," he said.

Mary smiled and leaned forward to shake his hand. "Mary," she said.

"Pleased to meet you, Mary. And you can call me...Wilbur," he said, and laughed. "Just please don't call me Will."

"Okay," Mary said. "Why not?" She was relaxing into the seat, looking out the windows, and enjoying the coolness of the car.

"Because I've spent my entire life—I'm twenty-seven now, by the way—getting used to hearing that name, and I'm almost there. Besides, when people start calling me Will they think my name is William, and I don't want to disappoint them by telling them what it really is."

No, Mary thought, this isn't going to be anything like the drive from the airport.

"You're not from around here, are you?" Wilbur asked.

"No, I'm not," Mary said cautiously. "How can you tell?"

The obvious answer would have been, "Because you're staying at a motel," but Wilbur said, "Oh, there's a particular look to the locals, and you don't have it."

And Mary wanted to ask, What look is that? White? But she didn't, because she never wanted to victimize herself and despised it when other people allowed themselves to be victimized. Not because it smacked of self-pity, but because it was self-destructive, and she refused to hurt herself. Sometimes. In fact, she did victimize herself on occasion. Not often, but enough. And, of course, it was always easier to find fault with others than find the same fault with yourself. As Mary well knew.

"Where are you from?" Wilbur asked.

"New Jersey," she said, but her voice was stiff.

"Okay. I've been there once."

"Did you like it?" Mary asked, sounding more anxious than she expected to.

"It was all right," Wilbur said, and again Mary thought he might have been overwhelmed or offended by the multiculturalism she didn't see around her there, but she hadn't really seen any "there" yet.

As soon as they left Jorgensen, everything started to disappear. Nothing but miles of very flat land with only the occasional farm in the distance. Everything was in the distance, nothing was near the road. When Mary had visited Las Vegas, when she was in college, she was taken aback by the lack of attractions (stimuli, really) between towns. Unlike New Jersey, where one was never far from some group of buildings—houses with no land around them, office parks, shopping centers—or, if one were traveling on a highway, multiple exits and overpasses.

"So what do you do?" Wilbur asked.

"I'm a classical pianist," Mary said. Talking about herself, she felt more relaxed. She preferred describing herself as a *classical* pianist rather than a *concert* pianist, because she found that term inflated. And it would always leave people asking, "Oh. Classical music?"

"Very cool," Wilbur said, and he sounded genuinely interested, which Mary found more appealing than him sounding genuinely impressed. Again, she never tried to impress people and often felt guilty when she did. "Me? I'm a driver for Four Kings. At least for now." Again he laughed, and Mary thought he must have felt comfortable with himself.

"Well I'm glad, because otherwise I'd wonder why the hell you were driving me somewhere," she said.

And after a moment Wilbur laughed, as though he had to think about what Mary said, and then, suddenly quieting himself, he said, "Okay. Serious question now."

"Yes?" Mary asked nervously.

"Maryann didn't send you, did she?"

"Maryann who?"

"Maryann Sims," Wilbur said, as though it were the most obvious answer in the world. "My wife."

Mary felt anxious. "I'm sorry," she said, swallowing. "Why would your wife send me?" She half-expected him to start slowing down and pull off to the side of the road. She had no idea what might follow.

Wilbur let out a sigh that implied both relaxation and relief. "Um. Well," he said, and rubbed his right middle finger across the bridge of his nose, moving his glasses. "She thinks I pick up women."

Mary was scared. "How much farther is Jinete College?" she asked.

"Are you worried?" Wilbur asked. "You sound worried."

Mary thought that only people who meant others harm said things like that. And he didn't sound sympathetic.

Then he slammed his right hand on the top of the steering wheel—he was driving with his left—and screamed, "Oh my God!"

And Mary jumped. He might have just slammed on the brakes. "What?!"

Wilbur started to laugh hysterically. "I'm sorry," he said. "I really am. No. Really. When I said my wife thinks I pick up women, she means for me to have sex with, not to murder them or anything."

Mary felt helpless and blamed it on not being remembered anymore, though if she had thought about it more rationally, she would have realized that being forgotten had nothing to do with it. Wilbur was a stranger who never knew her.

"And when you said your name was Mary, I figured you made it up, because Maryann is my wife's name, so if she'd sent you, you might have not wanted to use your real name, but choose a shortened version of Maryann."

But that, too, made her think that if she weren't forgotten, she might have been recognized, and Wilbur would know he was transporting a celebrity and, so, would treat her with the appropriate amount of respect.

A few minutes of silence followed. Then Wilbur asked, "It's a nice day, isn't it?" He sounded calm again, the way he had when she'd first gotten into the car.

Mary looked out the windows. The sun was shining, she was still comfortably cool, though her heart was racing, and she saw a town coming up. "Yes," she said bleakly.

"I'm sorry," he said. "I didn't mean to scare you. Yagoda is just about five miles ahead, so figure we'll be there in ten minutes."

That made her comfortable.

"It's just that she, Maryann, gets so damned jealous. And, I can promise you, for no reason at all. I've never done anything untoward to a woman. Not even to my wife."

Mary just wanted to get out of the car. She thought about unbuckling her seatbelt, throwing open the door, and jumping, but she doubted she would survive the jump. And Wilbur would only come back for her. There were no woods for her to run into. But realizing how ridiculous the idea was, she laughed.

"Did I miss something?" Wilbur asked.

"What do you mean?" She was becoming irritated. Of course, she thought, she was getting closer to the college, so she could afford to become irritated.

"You were laughing. I was just curious what you were laughing about."

To Mary, being afraid was a way of hurting herself, and that was something, as I said, she tried never to do. Yes, fear served a purpose—it could prevent people from putting themselves in jeopardy—but she knew, or thought she knew, when a situation really was threatening and when it wasn't. She attributed that to spending time alone and observing people objectively. Excessive emotional involvement blunted one's appreciation of danger.

She leaned forward and said, "Well that's the thing about comedy, you see. Not everybody finds the same things funny. And, I'm sorry, but I don't think you would find what I was laughing at funny, so I'm not going to share it with you. Is that all right, *Wilbur*?"

He shrugged. "Yeah, fine," he said. And for a few minutes, neither of them said anything. "So getting back to my wife," Wilbur said. "If she had her way, she'd probably keep me on a leash."

But before he could say "But I'm not into that," Mary tightened her lips, shook her head, and finally shrugged, then closed her eyes and positioned herself as though she were going to sleep. She knew she'd be dropped off at the college soon—she hoped she would—but she was sure that Wilbur was looking at her in the rear-view mirror, and she hoped that if he saw her like that, he'd stop talking.

And he did, until they got to Yagoda, five minutes later, at which time he said, "Well, here it is. We're in Yagoda now. Pretty town."

Driving up South Rapids Road toward Eberle Street, Mary looked out and watched the town unfold itself. She felt more impressed than she thought she would, but at that point anything would seem impressive, because her ride was almost over. She then noticed that the car smelled uncommonly good, like vanilla.

"Where would you like me to deposit you?"

"*Deposit* me?" Mary asked. "Oh, I'm sorry. In front of the Student Center, please."

"Sure," Wilbur said. "And I know just where it is, so give me a second and I'll let you off there."

Wilbur pulled up in front of a large brick building with an enormous flight of wide concrete stairs before its main entrance—to the left there was a wheelchair ramp—stopped the car, and let Mary out. And as soon as she stepped out and paid Wilbur, she felt not so much relieved as satisfied, which surprised her. Though, of course, she could then put the whole experience behind her. The ride to the college had been comfortable and smooth, and the conversation at very least interesting. And her worst fears hadn't come true. She wondered what her father would have made of it, and decided that he would have considered it just one more inconvenience to be endured, that would thus be followed by something much better—perhaps her concert would be a spectacular success—and she liked that.

"If you need a ride back—," Wilbur said, but she'd already walked away.

The Student Center was open, spacious, and barren. The plaster walls were painted white, the stucco ceilings were painted white, and the floor was covered in terrazzo tiles, also white, but with specks of gray. It was so highly polished that Mary was afraid she would slip if she walked too quickly. She saw a reception desk a few hundred feet in front of her, and if she looked straight ahead and narrowed her gaze, that would have been the only thing in her line of vision. A young man named Nathaniel was sitting behind it. She approached him. "Excuse me—," she said, and

Nathaniel, who had strawberry blond hair and a pockmarked face, said, "Oh my God. It's you," and smiled.

And Mary, more by instinct than any desire to appear modest, turned around quickly, then said. "Oh, you're talking to *me*."

"You're Mary Sorabi," Nathaniel said, and stood up. He was wearing a yellow checked, short-sleeve linen shirt with a cutaway collar, and blue jeans without a belt. She wondered if he was going to extend his hand the way Wilbur had, but he didn't. "You're appearing at the Elliott tonight."

She laughed. "Yes, I guess I am. How did you know?"

He pointed his right index finger at her, then moved it to the left. "Look," he said.

And on the wall, about fifty feet away, she saw a poster that read:

ONE NIGHT ONLY!

Saturday, May 22, 20—

MARY SORABI, pianist

First-Prize Winner of This Year's

Graffman International Piano Competition

Performing Works by Prokofiev, Schoenberg, and Ravel

She laughed at how much smaller the names of the composers were than her name was. Well, she thought, people were coming to see her, not to listen to the kind of music she played. Sad. And on the poster, between the line that listed the date and the line that listed her name, was her picture; the famous one, the one that would be replicated for years, long after she didn't look like that anymore.

"I really don't know what to say," she said, and forced a smile.

Nathaniel smiled back, but more naturally, jutting out his chin. "Don't say anything. Just let me know how I can help you."

This, she was convinced, was the reaction she'd been waiting for, only it didn't feel at all like she thought it would. And maybe that was because there wasn't a single other person there, so it had no resonance. Amazingly, the absence of people didn't strike her as strange.

"I'm looking for a man named Steve Manillo. I'm supposed to meet him—"

"I know," Nathaniel said, and nodded quickly. "Give me one second, please." He sat down, picked up his telephone, pressed a few buttons, and said into it, "Hey, Steve. She's here." And then, after a pause, "All right. I'll let her know."

Placing the phone down, he crossed his arms on the desk in front of him and leaned forward. She noticed that his lips moved very little when he talked. "When you first walked in here, you passed a set of stairs in the entryway. Walk up those stairs, and when you get to the second floor, walk down the hallway about halfway, until you see a door on your left that says Conference Room A. Don't worry. There won't be anyone in there, in spite of its name, except him."

But on her way up she felt odd, as though she'd stepped into a dreamworld. The swathes of emptiness that surrounded her seemingly everywhere she went were suddenly starting to pall.

Upstairs, she knocked on the door to Conference Room A.

"Come in," Steve said.

Mary opened the door a little and stuck her head in. "Steve?"

"Yes," reassuringly. "Mary?"

"Yes," Mary said. "I recognize your voice." She stepped in.

The room, which was remarkably small for a conference room, held a single oak table and two black plastic chairs set diagonally opposite each other. Steve sat in the one facing the door. He was a man in his middle forties, tall and thin, with dark brown hair that was groomed so impeccably she figured he'd just gotten it cut. He wore a light green button-down shirt, olive green slacks, and a tan sweater vest, much too heavy for that time of year. Where had he come from? What concerned Mary, though, was the fact that his face was so featureless, even generic, that she knew she would forget it a minute after she left, and not be able to recognize him again.

"Where is everybody?" she asked.

"I'm here," he said.

Mary laughed. "No, I mean—"

"Oh, the students?" Steve asked. "It's the end of the semester. Some have gone home and the rest are probably cramming for their finals."

Mary looked disappointed. "So there's going to be nobody at tonight's concert."

Steve imitated her dour expression. "It's sold out."

"No, seriously," Mary said, without smiling.

"I am being serious," Steve said, and then smiled. To Mary he looked like the kind of person who smiled too often, but hadn't yet learned how to make it convincing.

She shook her head. "Amazing," she said quietly. "I don't know what to say."

Steve sat back. "You're not used to it." He extended his right palm, facedown, and waved it gently. Mary knew he was telling her to sit, but she preferred to stand. "Don't worry," he said. "That'll come. So have you thought about how you want to spend your time today?"

"I figured I'd go to the art museum first, to relax." But relaxing wasn't why Mary wanted to go. She wanted to be reminded of her trip to the Philadelphia Museum of Art the day after her win, and feel confident and secure in preparation for that night's recital.

Steve squinted. "That's fine," he said, "but don't you want to check out the theater first?"

"Of course," Mary said. "I didn't know if I could."

"You could," Steve said and chuckled, though she found his muted laughter demeaning. "Can. It's all yours. Come with me, and I'll walk you there."

So they set out across the campus. Paved paths connected the various buildings that surrounded the broad lawn like a New England village green.

"Where is the theater?" she asked.

"Just ahead and to the left," Steve said, and pointed to it. It's caddy corner to Beveridge Hall."

And Mary thought, Is it just me, or do other people see the irony in having a building named Beveridge Hall right next to a theater?

The Rosalind Elliott Theater was a squat, circular building. It was obvious that the various buildings on the campus had been constructed at different times. Either that or they were designed to look that way. If the style of architecture was anything to go by, "the Elliott," as Nathaniel had called it, would have been erected in the 1930s or 1940s, though given that the college had been founded in 1865—Mary remembered seeing that on their website—it was sobering to believe that it took seventy years for a theater to be built. Unless it replaced an older one.

"Nice," Mary said, walking in. The floor in the lobby was covered with the same white terrazzo tile that she'd seen in the Student Center, though it seemed less slippery than the Student Center floor, which made Mary believe that it got more traffic. Maybe a herd of people had come through that morning to buy whatever tickets were left for her recital.

"There you are," Steve said, pointing to the sign of her that she'd seen earlier, and for a moment she felt, uncomfortably, that he was about to put his hand on her shoulder. *No touching, please.*

"That's me," she said, and walked over to it. She felt good, though a couple of feet to its right was another poster of similar size, announcing that the following Saturday night the theater would be hosting Roger Bittles, who would be reading from his new book, *Spit of the Cobra*. She'd never heard of Roger Bittles, so it didn't mean anything to her that his book was new, but, given how things were going, she hadn't been sure that anyone had heard of her, either, so she wished him well.

"Let's step inside first, so you know what it looks like. Now understand, the theater is closed; off limits to everyone except you and me and the people who work here. So if you want to practice, you'll have the entire place to yourself, and you don't want anyone to get a sneak preview of what's coming."

He opened the door to the theater and, standing beside it, said, "Come on in."

Everyone into the pool.

If the building in which they stood had been put up in the first half of the last century, the auditorium itself must have been refurbished within the past decade, because it looked notably new, and that look of newness was emphasized by its contrast with the lobby. The seats seemed unusually plush, in a dark blue fabric that Mary found beautiful, and the walls were ribbed oak, which, she knew, would afford good acoustics. Okay, she thought. I can get excited about this.

"It only seats three hundred seventy-five people," Steve said, "and there's no balcony or mezzanine, but I think, for a piano recital, that's a nice, intimate number."

"Intimate, yes," Mary said, first feeling disappointed—she should have asked before how large the theater was—but then acquiescent. She didn't say anything to Steve, but she wished he hadn't shown her the seats in the theater. She didn't like looking at the stage from the stalls, because then she'd think about what the audience might see and what they might think of her. As long as she was looking at the audience, she felt more in control.

"Come, we'll walk to the dressing room, then you can get out on stage and settle in. What motel did you say you were staying in?"

"The Tellory Inn in Jorgensen."

Steve laughed. "Yes," he said. "I was booked there, too, as Mel must have told you, but after I saw how far from the college it was, I changed my reservation to something much closer. I'm sorry, I should have thought about changing your reservation, too."

"Or spoken to Mel about it," Mary said, as much because booking their accommodations appropriately was Mel's responsibility, as because she thought Steve was becoming too familiar with her. But, again, when one isn't interested in relationships, one believes that that's all everyone else thinks about. Still, she asked, "So what motel are you in now?"

"I'm staying at the Four Points in Yagoda. Would you like me to see if I can book you a room there?"

"Thank you. No."

INTERVIEWER: Prokofiev or Shostakovich?

MARY: Why does it always have to be a contest? Prokofiev. He was a better composer for the piano, he was one of the great melodists of the twentieth century, and he was more versatile. But Shostakovich at his best, which was considerable and often, wrote deeper and, I suppose, *better* music. His *Twenty-four Preludes and Fugues*, which he based on Bach, is...*are?*...magnificent, and I think it's one of the greatest piano pieces of the last hundred or so years; maybe better than Prokofiev's ten piano sonatas combined. I think Shostakovich will outlast Prokofiev, but I like Prokofiev's music better.

INTERVIEWER (*Laughs*): Okay. Bruckner or Mahler?

MARY: Bruckner. But only by a little bit.

INTERVIEWER: Mozart or Haydn?

MARY: Definitely Mozart.

INTERVIEWER: Peaches or pomegranates?

MARY (*Laughs*): Peaches. I don't care for pomegranates.

INTERVIEWER: Clams or oysters?

MARY: Oysters.

INTERVIEWER: Dinner tonight?

MARY: Or not. Thank you, but no. I always eat by myself. Or at least prefer to.

"I've got all of my things there already. At my motel," Mary said. "And I'm leaving tomorrow morning, so it wouldn't pay."

Steve smiled. "Understood," he said.

"I'm also going to break for dinner, alone, at some point, after I practice."

He showed her to her dressing room. "Okay," he said, "this is how I think things should play out. You show up here at seven-thirty. I'll show you how to get in through the back entrance." He smiled. "You're not going to walk through the lobby because people would just mob you."

Was he being serious or making fun of her?

"And you want to show some sense of reserve." He had a more serious expression on his face. "Though that's not what I mean at all. I mean, whatever you're thinking, that's not it."

Until then Steve hadn't struck Mary as someone who got tongue-tied. He had his script rehearsed, well-rehearsed, and had been following it explicitly. "What I'm trying to say is, you're a celebrity, so you want to use your own private entrance and then come out on stage to appease the masses." He laughed again. "I can't believe I'm saying that, but you know what I mean. Your recital begins at eight. Half an hour should be enough time to get yourself settled, get your music together, if you use a score—"

"I do."

"And do whatever it is that relaxes you."

Mary laughed and turned to him. "I can't stand relaxing," she said, but didn't say anything more.

"Now I'm going to show you something special," Steve said.

She couldn't believe it, but she was missing Mel. Not missing the man, missing the familiarity.

Steve reached into his briefcase and extracted a printed program. "It's for your recital tonight," he said, and handed it to her, smiling. "It's all about you."

And she felt curiously touched. It was printed on heavy, glossy paper, replicated the picture of her that was on the poster, listed her program on one right-hand page, took several pages to explain the pieces that she would be performing, and, on half a page, gave her brief biography. The last several pages were filled with advertising. She thought about the descriptions of the music. Given that people were handed their programs as soon as they walked into the theater, and that many people walked in no more than five minutes before the performance began, who, exactly, would spend his or her time reading it? Perhaps it was something to refer back to afterward, but by then people's minds would be elsewhere.

"Come," Steve said, smiling again, "let me show you what it looks like."

And they walked onto the stage. For a moment Mary expected to hear welcoming applause but that, of course, didn't happen. The piano was a Steinway Model D, which Mary loved. She had a Steinway at home—much smaller, of course—and had tried and often played other pianos—Yamahas, a Bechstein, even a Bösendorfer—but she found the clarity, warmth, and glint of the Steinway best suited to the music she played.

She sat on the bench and looked out over the stalls. Steve stood about twenty feet behind her, so she couldn't see him.

"Play something for me," Steve said. "If you don't mind." Then added quickly, "And then I'll get Andrea out here. She'll be your page turner tonight. Her name is Andrea Solomon, and she's the best."

But his words sounded hollow, Mary thought. Praise often sounds hollow when it's phrased without the proper inflection, and Steve's voice carried no inflection whatsoever. She wondered, then, if he even knew what a page turner does and whether he knew anything about classical music. Maybe being an agent was just a job to him.

"So, all right," she said. "I don't have the music with me, but I'm going to play something that's in my head, and is a good piece to warm up with. It's my favorite of all of Chopin's etudes, the one in E minor, Op. 25, No. 5."

The tempo is marked *vivace*, which, in contrast to what many people think, isn't fast, and Mary began it slowly, to get a feel for the instrument, but quickly settled into the proscribed tempo, and was delighted to hear how good the instrument sounded. Before she got to the middle section she turned to Steve, smiled and nodded, and he said, "Yes, it's just been tuned," and she nodded again, though very slightly, wondering why anybody would talk during a performance, even if she was just practicing. Did he not know how to read cues?

"Very nice," Steve said, when she was done, and he did sound genuinely impressed.

"Okay, can I say something?" Mary asked.

"Of course."

"One thing that fascinates me about Chopin is that his earliest works, and this is not one of them, have a light, exquisite, refined quality that, to me, sounds very French. If you look at the eighteen nocturnes that he had published during his lifetime, you'll hear it immediately in the first, the B-flat minor. But as his music developed, he began to sound more Slavic, and the last nocturne, the beautiful E major, has a middle section that sounds positively Russian to me. But here's the thing. Have you ever heard Polish spoken?"

"I have not," Steve said.

"Well I have," Mary said. "And the language sounds like an exact cross between French and Russian. It's also the most beautiful language I know. So I guess that, in his music, Chopin was staying true to his roots."

"I guess," Steve said.

"You know what else I've noticed?" Mary asked. Steve shook his head. "The actual sound of a piano varies as much depending on my mood as on its acoustic. So when I'm feeling very happy, it sounds better to me than when I'm feeling sad."

"Makes sense," Steve said, then asked, sounding concerned, "How are you feeling now?"

"Good," Mary said. "Very good."

"Then you'll be great tonight," he said.

INTERVIEWER: What, to you, makes a performance *great*?

MARY (*After a pause*): That's a hard question to answer, because it depends on whether I'm performing or somebody else is. When I listen to a recording or somebody else performing live, my rule of thumb is that a *great* performance is any performance that can convince me that I'm listening to *great* music. And that isn't always the case. Sometimes I'll walk away from a performance and say to myself, Hmm, I thought Brahms, or Schumann, or Chopin, or whoever it was, was a much better composer than that. So that's really my only criterion for judging when someone else is playing. Whether the performer has convinced me that I've spent my time meaningfully and well.

INTERVIEWER: And what about when you perform?

MARY: When *I* perform? (*Pauses*) You want to know something? I'm going to tell you the same thing. But it's more complicated. Okay, first, I won't perform a piece of music that I don't believe in. Which is to say, a piece that I don't love or think is great. But I can step outside of myself, literally, and hear what I'm performing while I'm performing it, and wonder, Hmm, is she convincing me that this is great music?

INTERVIEWER: Are you harder on yourself or on other people?

MARY: Myself, of course. I've heard very few performances by others that haven't convinced me. But I've given a few performances that I know really weren't among my best. (*Pauses*) Several, actually. Too many.

INTERVIEWER: Did the audience enjoy them?

MARY: They seemed to, but I don't know. Maybe they were just being polite with their applause. But audiences are easier to please than I am, when it comes to the work I do. Which is why, as I told you before, I don't play for them, I play for myself. (*Laughs*) If I played for them I'd let myself get away with too much.

INTERVIEWER: Now stop me if I'm wrong, but if you're playing for yourself then the audience can basically go to hell.

MARY: I have an idea. Why don't you interview yourself? Then you can answer your own questions and interpret them any way you like. But as far as what you just said goes, the audience paid for their tickets, so they can go anywhere they please.

A few minutes later a young girl in a frumpy lime green cotton dress walked onto the stage, and Steve introduced her as Andrea Solomon. She was short, had bleach blonde hair cut in bangs, and buck teeth. But she seemed eager to help Mary, and they spoke for a while about the program Mary would be performing, with Mary going over each score with Andrea.

Then Steve announced that he would be heading back to the Student Center, so Mary knew where she could find him, and said, "And you have my number if anything comes up. Otherwise I'll see you back here at seven-thirty."

Andrea ended up showing Mary the back entrance to the theater.

At four o'clock Mary decided to break for dinner. Although she normally ate closer to six, and her performance was still four hours away, she liked eating long before she got out on stage, and trying to relax afterward.

She chose not to ask anyone where to eat—it was a recommendation, after all, that saddled her with Wilbur, though by then she could laugh about it—so she simply walked into town by following Lera Street to Eberle Street, to see what was around. The heat was starting to ebb, and the coolness came, not as a breeze, but as a suggestion. She knew the night would be chilly.

She settled on the Green Dragon, because she liked what they had on their menu, a copy of which had been taped to their front window. In such a small town, out in the Midwest, Mary thought, a Chinese restaurant would offer only the most basic and standard of Chinese dishes, which weren't even Chinese—chop suey, of course, moo goo gai pan, sweet and sour pork—but that was what most people were brought up on and taught to believe was Chinese. This restaurant had them, yes, but also offered hot and sour napa cabbage—she would have that as an appetizer—xialongbao, which was a type of dumpling filled, there, with crabmeat and pork—that was what she would have for her entrée—and, of course, her beloved char siu. It bothered her that she'd thought of a small town in Iowa as so parochial, but after a moment the bother was gone.

Walking back to the campus, she saw the sun setting and thought about how prolonged sunsets must be in areas of flat land. No trees or hills or, certainly, mountains obscured the sun before it sank below the horizon. Oddly, twilight was her least favorite time of the day. It was odd because the melancholy that it induced was the exact melancholy that she found so mesmeric in Brahms' music—the closing bars of the Third Symphony, she thought, captured that feeling perfectly—and because she loved the night more than the day, and twilight heralded it, let her know that something she adored was coming, so why should she have found it depressing?

Also, that time of the year could be hard for her. She lost both of her parents in May, though four years apart. Still, she had a concert to give that night, and that excited her. Her big moment, she thought, was about to begin.

When she walked out on stage, the applause that greeted her sounded much louder than she'd expected. It must be the acoustics, she said to herself, because she couldn't believe that fewer than four hundred people could generate that much sound, but maybe they were just excited and happy to see her. She'd changed into a long dark gray chiffon dress with a deep V-neck, and following a few steps behind her was Andrea, who had also changed, into a lavender skirt and blouse with rose frills.

But Mary didn't sit down at the piano. She stepped in front of it to address the audience. And once the applause stopped, she said, "Ladies and gentlemen," then bowed her head slightly, "I want to thank you so much for coming, and to welcome you to tonight's recital." She was nervous. She didn't mention it to Steve, because she knew he would call Mel, who'd tried to dissuade her from performing her "difficult" (for the audience to understand, not for her to perform) program, but she was reshaping it, adding more pieces so she could place the Schoenberg, which held the central position, in a more coherent context. Andrea already knew. "Tonight's program isn't going to be followed exactly as it's printed in the booklet. It's going to be embellished." And she heard sounds from the audience but wasn't sure what they were, so she couldn't tell whether the audience liked the idea or not. But she smiled, just hopefully, she thought, more authentically than Steve had. "So let me ask you first, how many of you are students here? You can let me know by a show of hands." And almost everybody's hand went up, after which there was laughter. "Excellent," she said, notably more relaxed. "Because I'm going to, I hope, teach you a few things about the music I'm about to perform." Then she added, though she knew she was running a risk by saying it, "If nobody has any objections." And that was followed by a round of applause and more laughter. "Wonderful," she said, looking down briefly, and stepping back. "Okay, so let me tell you what's now on tonight's program. I'm going to start with Handel's Harpsichord Suite in B-Flat Major, HWV 434. It's a short work in four movements, and the third of its four movements is marked 'Aria and Variations.' That aria was then used by Brahms as the basis of his own, very much larger, set of variations, which he called the *Variations and Fugue on a Theme by Handel*, Op. 24, so I'll play that next. Then I'm going to play one more work by Brahms, a very late work, his Intermezzo in E-Flat Minor, Op. 118, No. 6. This is one of his most oblique compositions, but it will be good to hear, because it will lead naturally into the next piece I'll play, which will be the Schoenberg, yes, *Schoenberg*," and everybody laughed, "Three Pieces, Op. 11, which was his first work for solo piano. Schoenberg, incidentally, loved Brahms, and there's more in common between their music than you might think. After that I'll play the scheduled Schoenberg Suite for Piano, Op. 25, and let you hear how Schoenberg handled the suite, which differs, of course, from how...

well," she laughed, "Handel handled it," and the audience laughed, too. "An intermission will follow," she said, "then we'll return to the key of B-flat major for Prokofiev's Eighth Piano Sonata, and finally finish with Ravel's magnificent *Gaspard de la nuit*, which bears a hidden relation to the Schoenberg Suite in that Ravel, like Schoenberg, used old forms into which he poured some very progressive ideas. I think you'll like it."

The audience chuckled a bit and applauded again, but too politely, she thought, and then she sat down and played the Handel suite. The work was only ten minutes long, but she was surprised and relieved to not hear any coughs or rustling of papers. There were signs all over the theater for people to turn off their cell phones.

After the Handel she got a fair amount of applause, less than she would have liked but more than she had expected, because Handel was hard to put across well on the piano. His keyboard music lent itself much less readily to the concert grand than Bach's did, and it didn't, in truth, show Handel at anything near his best. To be effective it needed to be performed on a harpsichord, the instrument for which it was written. But as soon as Mary began the Brahms, she heard "Ah"s when people recognized the melody that was about to be varied and embellished, as she'd just played it, in its original context, a few minutes before, and then she knew she'd made the right decision by arranging the program as she had. Building it in that way, it would have a cumulative impact, and not until the concert was over would the audience fully realize how much sense her programming made. She hoped.

In fact, she needn't have worried, because the Brahms, with its aureate conclusion, which could sound pompous for Brahms, if played primarily to impress, got her a tremendous round of applause and shouts of "Brava!"

Before she played the next work, the Brahms intermezzo, she said to the audience, "The next piece I'm going to play before we get to our scheduled program is the Brahms Intermezzo in E-Flat Minor, Op. 118, No. 6. It's a very short piece, lasting only about seven minutes, and it's very mysterious. At the end of his life, Brahms wrote twenty brief, aphoristic piano pieces, into which he concentrated his feelings of, perhaps, loss and regret, but also of wonder, the gratitude that, to the lucky among us, comes with age, and, as always with Brahms, nostalgia. After that I'll play the three similarly terse early pieces that Schoenberg grouped as his Op. 11, which, I think, you can hear as picking up where Brahms left off."

Then she played the Brahms, which, as she expected, left the audience hushed and, she hoped, awed. When she started the Schoenberg there was some discernible movement, but that was expected, she told herself, because the Brahms intermezzo, a mostly quiet piece, though with a loud, even violent, middle section, must have absorbed them so much that they were comfortable enough to relax when it was over. So she thought the noises she heard were an affirmation that the audience was enjoying itself. And when the Schoenberg piece was over, she heard the audience roar. Positively. Touched, she bowed humbly and held up the score. It wasn't me, she was saying, it was Schoenberg that you enjoyed. See? It *does* happen.

Once the applause died down, she stepped closer to the audience and grabbed her left hand with her right hand, which she then let drop in front of her. "Okay, the first thing I'd like you to do now, please, is close your eyes. Just for a second." She smiled. There seemed to be some discussion, or at least some grunting, but then most of the audience looked as though they'd closed their eyes. "And what I want you to think about is home. What your house looks like. Pick any room you want, and just think about it."

The audience went silent.

"Now open your eyes again, look around at the other people sitting in the audience, and tell me how many people had the exact same vision as you."

A few chuckles.

"Even if you're here with someone you live with, I can bet that you saw two completely different things. And just as everybody sees the same thing—their own home—differently, everybody is going to hear the same thing, in this case the Schoenberg Suite for Piano, Op. 25, which I'm going to perform next, differently." A collective but reassuring sigh. "And this is the first piece I'm playing tonight that was on the original program, so the three of you who came for it won't be disappointed."

General laughter.

"But here's why I asked you to do that experiment. Schoenberg, let's be honest, is a divisive figure. Some people, like me, love his music. Some people hate it. And most people, you may be surprised to know, remain completely indifferent. It's possible that more has been written about his music than about any other composer I can think of. And by 'written about,' I don't mean, necessarily, in scholarly articles. Which is a nice way of saying he has a reputation he needs to live down. So what I want you to do is think about your image of home and forget it. Let it go. It's neither right nor wrong, so just let it go. And think about your image of Schoenberg's music and let *that* go, too. And now listen to what he wrote, and let me know what you think."

And before Mary put her fingers on the keys she heard another resounding "Brava!" from the audience, and more applause than what had greeted her when she'd first walked onto the stage. She knew she had them.

She smiled, turned to them, and said, "It's Handel through a kaleido-scope." Then immediately began the präludium, and was convinced she'd never heard an audience so quiet. There followed the gavotte, musette, intermezzo, menuett, and gigue. And once again the audience was in an uproar. They'd actually enjoyed the Schoenberg Suite.

"Now before we break for our intermission," Mary said, "I just want to explain something, and then I'm going to shut up," a smattering of laughter, "because I don't really need to introduce the Prokofiev or the Ravel that you'll hear later. Your program book does an excellent job of that." She assumed. She wanted to add, "And since you bought your tickets knowing what would be played, there's no reason for me to explain it to you," but she didn't because, after all, she had no idea why anyone bought their tickets. Again, it could have been because they had nothing better to do.

"Bach, who was Handel's exact contemporary, understood mathematics and used it in his music, by which I mean, he applied a strict and rigorous method of composition, because the Lutherans believed that mathematics was one of man's closest approaches to the perfection of God. Schoenberg did the same thing, which is to say, took a strict and rigorous means of composition, and applied it to *his* music, but he's derided for it. Maybe because his music is felt by some to be 'cold,' but I find it hyper-emotional. Not pretty, but not all emotion is going to caress. So think about that the next time you hear a piece by Schoenberg. And I hope there is a next time. I'll see you after intermission."

And the audience stood, but not to leave; to applaud her.

Mary and Andrea walked back to the dressing room, where Steve was standing with an enormous smile on his face. "Oh, my God, Mary, you hit it out of the park."

Mary laughed because she thought a sports analogy seemed so out of place under the circumstances, but she blushed, too, and bowed her head. "This is what you get when you do something you love," she said.

"And your audience—I'm not going to say *the* audience, I'm going to say *your* audience, because you own them—loved it, too."

But Mary didn't like that. She was glad, of course, that the audience reacted as well as it did—"well" in the sense of "desirably"—but she didn't want to own them, she wanted to be devoted only to the music, not to the other people who were listening to it. "Is there a problem with our running over?" she asked. The music she'd added to the first half of the program, to say nothing of her talking, extended her recital by more than an hour.

Steve pursed his lips and shook his head. "No," he said. "Not at all. We've got all night." Then he laughed. "No one needs the space after we're done."

Mary, as she'd promised, didn't talk to the audience during the second part of the program, when she played the Prokofiev and the Ravel. In the long-ago, or not-so-long-ago, days, performers never spoke to an audience. There was something like a class difference between them; the performer—elevated—and the audience—lowered. The performer was the authority. He or she knew everything he or she needed to know about the music that was being played, and the audience, hopefully, ideally, could appreciate some of it. The performer was lavishly attired, but audiences rarely dressed up for concerts. Mary didn't like that. Ironically, because, to her, the music was more of a priority than the audience was, but this just showed how one could take an ostensibly noble intention that other people might find haughty, and, in effect, use it to please everybody.

That was one reason why she didn't play the Prokofiev last. Its cataclysmic conclusion was maybe too geared to bring an audience to its feet. If, of course, it's played well, and it's a difficult piece to perform. But after the Prokofiev and after the Ravel she got her thunderous applause and, at the end, a standing ovation. The audience simply wouldn't quiet down, and when somebody, or maybe it was a few people, or even several, she didn't know, shouted, "We love you, Mary!" she again held up the score, that time to the Ravel, to let them know that her concert was about the music, not her performance, not her. She'd held up a score before, but by doing it a second time, and that time in response to the words that had been yelled, she was letting the audience know exactly what it meant. *Shift your focus, people.*

Then the audience shouted for an encore, and after Mary and Andrea walked off the stage and returned, the audience shouted louder, so Mary played, announcing what it was, the Brahms Intermezzo in C Major, Op. 119, No. 3, the piece that she was about to practice when she first met the judges. Well that seemed wholly appropriate, Mary thought, and smiled.

And for the last time, the audience was on its feet. But then, while she was listening to the final applause ringing throughout the theater, refusing to die, the acoustics changed. Suddenly the applause sounded louder and sharper, clearer, and she knew exactly what happened. The judges had reversed their decision. She wasn't forgotten anymore. She was known, remembered. And later, when she looked at her cell phone, she saw four calls from Mel, three calls from Leila, one call from Lizzy, one call from Julietta, and a text from Mel that said "Brava. You own this town. You're going to own many towns." Evidently Steve had been in touch with him.

Walking back into the dressing room, she noticed something strange. Steve looked different. And so did Andrea. There was a mole, or perhaps it was just a birthmark, in the shape of a club on a playing card, just beneath Steve's left eye. How could she not have noticed that before? And Andrea no longer had buck teeth. At least they didn't look buck to Mary. She had no idea what was going on, but she would talk to the judges about it, and remained happy.

"Anyone up for a nightcap?" Steve asked.

But the question sounded genuine, optimistic, not threatening. Still, Mary wouldn't have been Mary if she'd said yes, so she explained that she needed to get back to the motel because she had an early flight the next day—she didn't; it left at twelve o'clock—but she thanked him and promised she'd take him up on his offer the next time, knowing, of course, that she would never see him again. However, she needed a ride back to Jorgensen. "Does anybody know the quickest way for me to get there?" she asked.

"Call Uber," Steve said. "I can do it for you."

"Okay," Mary said. "Just as long as it's not Four Kings."

"Who?" Steve asked distractedly.

Mary laughed. "Four Kings," she said. "They're a car service, and they're terrible."

Then Andrea asked, "Really?! I've lived here all my life and I use car services all the time, and I've never heard of them."

And Mary thought, Of course.

When she got back to her motel she walked through the lobby, and Ernie said, "Hey-ho, Ms. Sorabi!"

She looked at him with a blank expression on her face.

"I hear you wowed them tonight."

Mary was confused. "You know me?" she asked.

"Of course," Ernie said, nodding. "Well, not personally, but it isn't every day we have a celebrity staying with us."

"Tell me," Mary said, "is there someplace I can get a glass of tomato juice?"

Ernie puckered his lips. "The restaurant is closed, but I'll have a glass sent up to your room."

"Thank you," she said, and walked upstairs.

In bed that night she read ten short stories by Saki. Wonderfully amusing and always deeply insightful. And when she looked out her window before drawing the drapes—her room faced a row of parked cars beyond which were only fields—she relished the quiet and the solitude, and even felt sad that she would be going home the next day to a world that would be much busier.

The Uber driver who drove Mary to East Iowa Airport was not the man who'd driven her to the hotel, but, like him, said only "Hello" and "Thank you." Her trip to Iowa, she realized then, had come full circle.

On the flight to Philadelphia, Mary had an interesting realization. She was thinking back to what she'd told her audience about how different people hear things differently, because everybody's points of reference are unique. And she was extemporizing then; she hadn't planned to say that, it just came to her. And while she was flying, she thought about how, one day, while playing through Schumann's *Kreisleriana*, she realized that she didn't understand the music at all. It didn't touch her, it didn't move her, and that bothered her because it was considered "important," "great," and absolutely "typical" of a composer she otherwise adored. So she tried to imagine what was running through Schumann's mind when he wrote it, hoping that by putting the music in its original context, she could understand it better. But she didn't. Until, some time later, while playing through it again, she realized that she never could and never would know what Schumann was thinking, not because she never *knew* him but because she never *was* him. You can know someone as intimately as you like, but you'll never really know what's running through his or her mind, because everybody's thoughts are locked away; cloistered. So she started going through her own thoughts, letting the music conjure memories of people and places she knew and remembered, and by doing so the music started to reveal itself, with certain phrases and certain passages evoking images from her past that meant a lot to her. And finally, she realized, *Kreisleriana* did touch her and did move her, and that was when she understood the magic of how music communicates.

The flight lasted almost four and a half hours, with the, by then, obligatory layover in Chicago, and it was a quarter after six when she finally opened her front door. Immediately, though, she heard the whistle, so she walked quickly into the living room to see the judges, to whom she said, "I'm going to need a little time to unpack and get myself settled in, if you don't mind, and the first judge nodded and said, "Please," but meaning that it was all right, that they didn't mind being kept waiting, not that they needed to discuss anything with her immediately.

She had only one valise, a garment bag, and a toiletries bag with her, so it didn't take her long, then she walked back to the living room, smoothed out her skirt, sat on the piano bench, and smiled. The judges, of course, couldn't smile back, and the snow fell in their chasms as it always did, but she was excited because she wanted to hear the good news and to ask them some questions about what had gone on.

The first judge sat up as erectly as he could, and said, "See, the Conqu'ring Hero Comes."

"From *Joshua*," the second judge said. "By Handel. As I'm sure you know, and which, under the circumstances, seems entirely appropriate."

Then, after a pause, the third judge said, "We're sorry, we don't sing," and all four of them laughed, with Mary realizing that she'd never laughed with the judges before.

"Can we have the projector, please?" the first judge asked.

The light in the brass lamp went out and Mary saw the projection screen and slide projector, with the little felt cups around its feet, on the cocktail table.

"We don't even know where to begin," the second judge said, "but you performed magnificently."

"'Performed,'" the third judge said, "and 'performed.'"

"First slide, please," the first judge said, pulling up the cuff on his left pants leg, and Mary saw a picture of the Uber driver who picked her up at East Iowa Airport. "Exhibit A. This is Carlos Fortunato. You never knew his name, did you?"

"No," Mary said, biting her lower lip. "I didn't."

"Are you surprised to know that there are people named Carlos who live in Iowa?" the first judge asked.

Mary blushed, shifting slightly. "Should I be?" she asked.

"*Should* you be? No. *Are* you? Perhaps. Next slide, please, Mr. Slide-Advancer."

And Mary saw a picture of Wilbur. "Oh, Wilbur," she said, and laughed, happy that she could.

"You're laughing, because you understand it now, don't you?"

"I do," Mary said, leaning forward. "Or at least I think I do."

"You do," the second judge said calmly. He crossed his legs.

"Wilbur," the first judge said, "has issues. Possibly many issues." He laughed. "But not necessarily more than anybody else has."

"Wilbur," the third judge said, and shook his head.

"What's most important," the first judge said, "is that you handled yourself well."

"Even swimmingly," the third judge said.

"Swimmingly?" the second judge asked, turning to him.

The third judge shrugged. "I thought it fit."

The first judge leaned back. "Next slide, please, Mr. Slide-Advancer."

And there was a picture of Steve, with his birthmark readily apparent. "Okay, stop," Mary said, leaning forward and looking confused.

"What's wrong?" the second judge asked, leaning forward himself.

Mary exhaled loudly. "That birthmark. Is it real?"

"Of course it's real," the first judge said, clasping his hands on his lap. "Why shouldn't it be? It doesn't come and go."

"But I didn't—," Mary said, raising her right arm slightly.

"See it?" the first judge asked. "No, you didn't. But it was there all along. Mary, you didn't see it because you were keeping your distance from him, and when people keep a distance, they miss things."

"Which is not a criticism of your keeping your distance," the second judge said, raising his right index finger and shaking it as though he were putting out a match. "All we're saying is that the closer you get to someone or something, the more you see. Or, rather, the more you're able to see."

"I understand that," Mary said, looking perturbed, "but I was the same distance away from him when I saw it as when I didn't see it."

"Okay, think of it this way," the second judge said, sitting back. "Have you ever had a problem that you just couldn't figure out, no matter how hard you thought about it? And then, suddenly, the answer came to you, and you thought, 'Of course! How obvious! Why didn't I think of that before?'"

Mary shook her head and laughed. "Lots of times," she said. Then she swung her right leg, which surprised her.

"Well, one reason you might not have thought of it is that the answer scared you. But you didn't realize that. So you avoided answering it. Then, once you realized that the answer wasn't so threatening after all, you were able to embrace it. And that's exactly what happened here. Steve scared you. You thought he was trying to come on to you. So you avoided him and avoided seeing what he really looked like. And that's understandable. You were an unknown to him before the concert. He might have had ideas. I'm not saying he did and I'm not saying he didn't; I don't know. But he might. But then, after the concert, when he realized who you were, and started showing you more respect, you no longer felt threatened, so you were able to see what was right in front of you, and that was Steve and his birthmark."

"As you yourself said in your interview," the third judge said, "and I quote, 'people don't hear what's in front of them, they hear what's in their minds.'"

"And they *see* the same way, too," the second judge said.

"When you think about people differently, you see them differently," the first judge said. "And that's not just a figure of speech."

Mary shook her head. "Okay," she said, "So what about Andrea's buck teeth that weren't buck?"

"Oh, they were," the first judge said, leaning back and relaxing, "and still are. But you had no reason to think about them after you realized she wasn't a threat. So you stopped seeing it."

And the second judge said, "When you perceive somebody as a threat, you look to find flaws with him or her to make them less intimidating."

"A threat? How did I see her as a threat?" Mary asked.

The third judge cleared his throat. "She was walking onto the stage with you, possibly stealing some of your glory. But think about why she was there. She was turning the pages for you. She was doing something you knew needed to be done. She was vital to the success of your concert. So," he said and shrugged, "because you understood how much you needed her, you saw her as a threat. A threat because you either knew you couldn't have gotten through the concert without her, or didn't want to get through the concert without her."

"You wouldn't have felt nearly as confident without her," the first judge said, crossing his arms, but resting his elbows on his lap. "So the fear that she would suddenly leave you became a threat."

"And Wilbur," Mary said, tensing. "Was he real?"

The first judge laughed. "Of course he was real. Mary, please understand, we're not magicians. We can't create apparitions for our own benefit."

"Nor would we want to," the second judge said.

"And," the first judge said, "none of this is being done to teach you anything, though if you're learning from it, that's wonderful. All we're doing is showing you how you really see the world."

"And that's neither good nor bad," the second judge said.

The third judge shook his head and repeated, "Neither good nor bad," and his voice sounded almost musical.

"Next slide, please, Mr. Slide-Advancer," the first judge said. But that was a picture of Andrea, and as she'd already been discussed, the third judge forwarded to the slide after that. That showed Mary standing on the stage, explaining to her audience the change in the program.

"Now here we have to applaud you," the first judge said, first leaning forward then sitting back. "Clap, everybody," and all three judges clapped politely. Then the three judges and Mary laughed. "This was you at your best."

"Sadly, one's best doesn't come that often," the third judge said. "To most people."

"Now Mel," the first judge said, "had urged you strongly to change your program. Next slide, please, Mr. Slide-Advancer." And there was a picture of Mel, sitting behind his desk, doing what he'd told Mary he never did: trying to smile but looking like he was smirking.

"Did he say that because he didn't know me?" Mary asked. She looked around her as though something else had caught her attention.

"That's a good question," the first judge said. "I don't know."

"You don't *know*?" Mary asked. "I thought you knew everything. That was how you're able to judge."

The second judge let his shoulders drop. "Mary, people judge all the time, and often, too often, with far less information about what they're passing judgment on than we have. No, we don't know everything. We know only what's presented to us, and that's how we're able to formulate our decisions."

"So as I was saying," the first judge said, sounding a little irritated, "I think you can figure out better than we can why Mel thought you should change your program. But remember what he does and think about what you do. Your objectives are not the same."

"Understood," Mary said quietly. She wished the first judge would ask "Mr. Slide-Advancer" to change the picture, because she couldn't stand looking at Mel, especially with the smirk on his face.

"But you did something extraordinary," the first judge said. "You played the program you wanted to play."

"And let me tell you something," the second judge said, "and I'm sorry for interrupting." He turned toward the first judge, who then shook his head, and for a moment Mary thought they were all going to tip back their hoods, if that's what they were, and reveal themselves to be real people. "When the audience applauded at the end, it was as much for you not compromising your integrity as for the quality, the *considerable* quality, of your performance."

Mary smiled and said, "Thank you," though she didn't necessarily believe it.

"They were students," the first judge said, "and you taught them. You taught them how to appreciate what you were doing, and by doing that, you were showing them respect. Feeling and accepting that respect, they listened more closely and more carefully to the music you were playing. It cut much deeper than it would have otherwise."

Then the second judge said, "I don't know if you realize this, Mary, or can realize it, but your concert, your recital, whatever you'd prefer to call it, changed at least one person's life."

"Whose?" Mary asked, suddenly animated.

The first judge shook his head and laid his left palm, facedown, on his lap. "It doesn't matter," he said. "Just be proud of it."

And the fact that Mary didn't repeat her question pleased the judges enormously.

"You made Mel look good, too," the third judge said.

"So in the end," the first judge said, "everyone triumphed."

"Now," the first judge said, resting his hands in his lap and leaning forward slightly, "just to keep things fair, I have to ask, is there any 'argument against'?"

The second and third judges looked at each other and shook their heads, then moved their heads closer and whispered.

"Maybe," the third judge said, turning forward, and sitting upright. "The concert did run over its allotted time, and that may have been an issue for anyone there who was following a schedule. Especially as virtually the entire published program started later, with two of the three pieces being played after intermission."

"Well normally—," Mary said, but the first judge gently waved his right palm, which meant she should please be quiet. What she'd wanted to say was that was that only one work, the Prokofiev, was played after intermission, rather than before, though the intermission did occur much later.

The first judge sat silent for a moment, then shook his head. "That's all right," he said. "I don't think anybody left during the entire performance, which is, in itself, unusual."

"And a tribute to your command of your craft," the second judge said, kicking his right foot slightly forward.

"Then we're in agreement and the judgment is now official," the first judge said.

"Agreed," the third judge said quietly.

Leaning forward, the second judge asked, "Did you enjoy it, Mary? Your trip to Iowa."

And Mary relaxed. "I did," she said. "More than I expected to."

"Will you go back?" the third judge asked.

"I don't know," Mary said, and a look of worry quickly passed over her face. "If they ask me. Will they?"

The first judge laughed and threw his arms in front of him. "Again, Mary, you're expecting too much of us. We can't tell the future."

"Nor would we want to," the second judge said, shaking his head.

"Not even close," said the third judge.

Then the screen disappeared, the projector was gone, and the light came back on.

"Then until we meet again," the first judge said and stretched. And then they all went silent.

Mary made herself a snack—a salad consisting of mixed greens, local tomatoes (she was told), red onions, avocado slices, radishes, and a champagne vinaigrette, with a glass of tomato juice—then went to bed early. She didn't listen to music, she didn't practice, she didn't read, and she didn't call anyone. All of that could wait for tomorrow.

In bed, she wondered if she would ever go back to Jinete College. She was sure Mel would tell her that they wanted, *demanded*, a return engagement, "though maybe not such a long program," Mary imagined him saying, and she laughed to herself. But maybe not. Maybe she would be disappointed to find out that the college had no interest in her coming back. What would really disappoint her, though, would be going there again and having little of the fun she'd had the first time. Though return engagements were often like that, and trying to replicate anything so perfect—yes, she thought; she could say that, in retrospect—was bound to fail. Which was why she had her memory, and that Saturday night in Yagoda, Iowa would always be embedded there. It was nice, she thought, to know how it felt to be a winner.

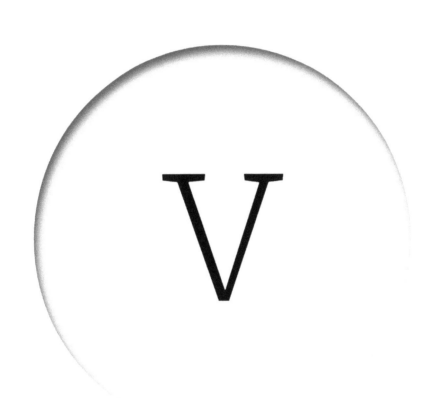

The signs had been up for weeks already, stapled or tacked or taped to telephone poles and electric poles all over town, and in most of the shop windows.

The Town of Ardell Presents:
Its Annual Memorial Day Weekend Event
SHELLEY THE DANCING CRAB
With Rhoda and Her Musical Friends
At the intersection of Shore Road and Coralis Avenue
PLUS:
Local Stores Will Be Open for a Sidewalk Sale!
Saturday, May 29, 20—
FESTIVITIES BEGIN AT 11:00 AM AND RUN THROUGH 5:00 PM

What the signs failed to mention, of course, was that both Shore Road and Coralis Avenue would be closed to vehicular traffic for at least four blocks in each direction, as that might have discouraged people who lived outside of town from driving in. But they would find out quickly enough, and municipal parking that day would be free.

Ardell hosted this event every year, and to some people it was what to look forward to. The intersection of Shore Road and Coralis Avenue would be roped off, and in the center of it a white, rectangular, plastic tub measuring twenty feet by ten feet by three feet deep, that was layered with silt and filled halfway up with seawater, would be set on risers, and in it would be a large adult female crab, Shelley, and a mound of sand onto which she could crawl. Standing in front of the tub would be Rhoda—she wasn't known by any other name—a redheaded woman in her early sixties, who wore too much makeup, thick, pasty, and white, and far too much lipstick, which was muddy green to match her slinky sequined dress and, by extension, Shelley, though Rhoda's dress never did match Shelley because Shelley was always paler. Shelley was also, needless to say, replaced each year, though whether, at the end of the festivities, she was released back into the ocean or eaten would never be made clear. To the left of the tub would be a man playing the banjo, whom Rhoda would occasionally refer to as Fred, behind the tub would be a man playing the trumpet, whom Rhoda would occasionally refer to as Wally, and to the right of the tub would be a man playing the harmonica, or mouth organ, though he sometimes switched to the accordion, and whom Rhoda would occasionally refer to as Gerald.

At the appointed time, the three musicians would start playing their instruments—they played jazz standards: *Body and Soul*, *All the Things You Are*, *Summertime*, and the like—while Rhoda, who would then be handed a long baton and a tambourine, would sing along with them. And her voice was good, at least in the sense that it didn't wobble, she sang on key, and she remained remarkably well coordinated with the three men around her. I say "remarkably," because one could tell, after listening to her for a minute or two, that she wasn't a professional singer. Nor was she a professional dancer, but she would strut, pirouette, spin, and gyrate as the music demanded, shaking and smacking her tambourine and then, on occasion, throw her baton to a man—always the same man—standing a few feet away from her, but not near the crowd that would invariably form, and he, in turn, would throw her, Frisbee-style, a straw boater, which she'd then catch, toss above her head twice, and raise and lower on top of her too-heavily coiffed henna-red hair in time to the music. After about fifteen minutes there would be a break, always announced, and though the lengths of the breaks varied, they were never longer than the time Rhoda and the musicians spent singing and playing, and then they would start up again. Remarkably, perhaps, they never played the same song twice.

But the star of the show was Shelley. Two men in starched white shirts and tight black pants would stand on the far sides of the tub and shake it between them, so that Shelley would "dance." Sometimes, when the men weren't shaking her tub, Shelley would climb onto the sand obliquely, and sometimes she wouldn't move at all, which would make people wonder if she was dead or just needed more water, but a lot of people who lived on the shore knew that crabs can stay out of water for as long as twenty-four hours. And yet, Shelley's stardom not withstanding, it was Rhoda and the three instrumentalists who the people came to see, to say nothing of the man—always the same man—who caught her baton and her hat and threw back whichever one he was holding. Shelley was there because it was the Jersey Shore, where a sometimes surprising number of crabs could be found. One didn't have to drive to Baltimore to see them.

Now Ardell was considered an upscale community, one that people thought of in the way they thought of Sea Girt, Avalon, and Stone Harbor, so it would seem one of the least likely places to host such a festivity, but that was why it had been launched, seven years earlier, by then-Mayor Elijah Parks, a former calculus professor at Rutgers University. He was afraid that people avoided shopping in, eating in, and visiting Ardell because it was too expensive—"There only the air is cheap," people used to say—so, by featuring an annual festival that he wanted to be "as tacky as possible," he could let people know that Ardell had another side. Well, of course it had another side; there was another side to everything. And, in truth, having a woman singing Gershwin could be considered at least a little upscale, but it became popular, and when, two years later, the shops along Shore Road and Coralis Avenue started hosting a sidewalk sale, the town became overrun with tourists, much to the chagrin of many of the locals, who preferred keeping their hamlet a bit less occupied by strangers and who, in fact, did not vote the mayor back into office.

"Are you going?"

Mary laughed. She was on the phone with Leila. "Lei-la," she said, drawing out the name.

"What?!"

"Do I have to?" she asked, again stretching her words, and laughing once more. She was laying on her bed, leaning slightly to the left. It was nine o'clock on Friday night.

"No, of course you don't," Leila said, "but it'll be fun."

"Fun for who? Whose idea of fun is this?"

"Oh, don't be such a wet blanket. Okay, you're going. What time should we be at your place?"

I no longer have a *house*, Mary thought. I have a *place*. She didn't like that. Too informal. "At two o'clock," she said.

"Two o'clock?" Leila asked. "Why two o'clock?"

"We'll grab a late lunch—"

"That's a *very* late lunch."

"And then we'll walk around town for a bit. I really don't want to spend that much time there."

"You know what a late lunch means, don't you?" Leila asked.

"Of course," Mary said. "It means I don't want to join you for dinner." And they both laughed.

"Well, think of it this way," Leila said. "Last weekend you were in college, this weekend you'll be in kindergarten."

"Nursery school," Mary said. But she was glad that Leila understood her. Mary didn't want to go, had never gone, though she knew about it, and always thought of it not just as something to avoid, but something to be proud of avoiding, though avoidance came easily to someone who preferred not to venture outside. For the past seven years she thought that the people who went to such things led frankly pitiful lives. There was no nice way to say it or for her to think about it. She tried to imagine what kind of people could enjoy something like that, but she couldn't, because Mary was never able to think that far outside of herself. Driving through Sitters by the Sea once, on her way to visit Leila, her eye had been caught by a very old house, more of a bungalow, really, with discolored white aluminum siding and pale yellow trim. She tried to imagine the lives of the people who lived there. At least that was what she told herself, but what she'd really tried to imagine was what her life would be like if she lived there. Her imagination could stretch only so far. And yet, as long as she was happy, and as long as she knew how to make and keep herself happy, who could complain? And I ask that sincerely. She never openly criticized people who didn't have what she had or didn't like what she liked. And being happy never made her feel superior, just blessed and fortunate. Besides, pity didn't hurt her, the way anger and hatred did.

Anyway, that year, when she thought it over, Mary decided that seeing Shelley the Dancing Crab might be fun. She'd never felt that way, but so much had changed in her life recently that she was excited to try one more new thing, and if she didn't like it, she could go back to feeling proud of herself for not going the following year. Mary did enjoy jazz—she had a German friend at NYU who pronounced it "yotz"—but usually when it was kept at a distance, when it added color, say, to a piece of classical music. Ravel used it in his piano concertos, Poulenc used it, even Debussy used it (what was it with the French and their love of jazz?), but she couldn't focus on it for very long because it was improvisational, and she liked, needed, demanded structure in whatever she exposed herself to.

Mary stood by her kitchen window that Saturday afternoon, waiting for Lizzy's car to pull up. It was hot and sunny. Lizzy and Julietta lived the farthest away, in Onica Lake, which was ten miles north of Ardell, and Leila, who they would pick up, lived in Sitters by the Sea, which was five miles north, so right between them. As a result, Leila's house was where they would meet most often when they got together. They hadn't all decided to live near each other when they were in college. Mary had lived in Ardell all her life, and Leila had lived in Mount Kisco, New York, but visited Mary often enough on school breaks and occasional weekends to know that when she moved out of her parents' house, she wanted to live on the Jersey Shore, which, until she met Mary, was someplace she'd never been. And since she was a translator, almost all of her business was freelance and conducted virtually, so she could live anywhere she wanted. Mary had told Leila that living somewhere was not the same as vacationing there, and that whatever charm the shore—or Mary's parents' house, which Leila thought of as palatial—might have had would be dispelled as soon as she moved there, but maybe Mary was just worried that Leila would occupy too much of her time.

Lizzy had lived in Metuchen but spent her first eleven summers at her maternal grandparents' cottage in Ocean City, so she, too, loved the shore. A year after graduation she found a job at an occupational therapy office in Atlantic City and, five years after that, finally bought a house in Onica Lake. And Julietta had lived in Flushing, Queens, and she, like Leila, had grown up without ever having visited the Jersey Shore. To New Yorkers, the shore was called "the beach," and the beaches she was most familiar with were Jones Beach and Watch Hill on Fire Island. But Julietta, like Leila, was a freelancer, so she could live pretty much anywhere she chose, and when Lizzy found herself a house in Onica Lake, Julietta found herself a modest garden apartment there, too.

Mary opened her front door when Lizzy's car pulled up, but saw only Leila and Lizzy get out. "Where's Julietta?" she asked, when they walked up to the house. She looked worried.

Leila smiled, threw her arms around Mary's shoulders, and laughed. "Hi, Mary. And it's good to see you, too." Leila was tall and svelte. She had dark brown hair that she wore in a bun, very narrow eyes, a long nose, and a wide mouth with large, exceptionally white teeth. Mary often saw Leila's features as an exaggerated version of her own, but she also thought Leila looked more worldly: grown-up, mature, and knowledgeable. There was nothing childlike or boyish about her.

Lizzy, as was her wont, just grinned and put up her right hand in a feeble wave. "She got involved with other things," she said. Lizzy was short, had red hair and pale white skin, a forehead dotted with freckles, a small, slightly droopy nose, like a baby owl's beak, and thin lips that she always curled. To Mary, Lizzy had a surprisingly expressive face, "surprisingly" because her demeanor was so impassive. She tended toward stockiness and had very thick fingers.

"So she's not coming," Mary said, and stepped back.

"She's going to meet us after lunch," Leila said, walking inside. Mary barely made room for her.

"Then she doesn't want to have lunch with us," Mary said, shaking her head, looking very serious, and staring at the floor.

"She doesn't want to have lunch with *you*," Leila said. "Mary, what's the matter? Is something wrong?"

"You know how Julietta is," Lizzy said, though without enthusiasm, so Mary couldn't tell if she were trying to make a point.

"I don't think she likes me," Mary said.

"Join the club," Leila said. "I don't think she likes anyone. Really, I don't."

"Well at least I asked," Mary said. Although Mary rarely invited people to her house, she wanted her friends to be there then, because the event they were going to was in town, and she wanted to know if they would see the judges when they stood in her living room and faced the couch. She'd been told that they wouldn't and couldn't, but Mary needed to find that out for herself. Leila had been calling her every night for three nights, telling her how badly she wanted to come over, so Mary was careful not to do or say anything out of the ordinary—in fact, she didn't even leave her house—so the judges would have nothing to judge her on. She wondered what would have happened if her friends had shown up during a session—she didn't want to call it a "trial," because it wasn't; it was just the handing down of a decision—but she thought the judges were more clever than that, and scheduled their talks only for times when they knew no one would stop by.

They walked into the living room. Leila sat on the center cushion of the couch, Lizzy sat in the recliner, and Mary sat on the piano bench. She waved her hands as if to stop Leila, but then saw that she settled in perfectly well. Staring at the couch she saw the judges, just as they'd said she would, but saw Leila sitting right on top of them, or, rather, over them. Superimposed. It was a very unsettling image, as Leila seemed to be sitting on the second judge's lap. "Sit back," Mary said, and Leila did so, which relieved the scene for Mary. For a moment Mary wondered if the second judge, the most amiable of the three, was going to grope her, and she let out a startled laugh, but, of course, the judges remained motionless.

"What I really think," Lizzy said. "Can you hear me from there?"

"Of course," Mary said, looking concerned again. "Why do you ask?"

"Because your living room is so damned big. No, what I really think is that Julietta doesn't trust anybody. I think she thinks people don't like her."

"Can't argue with that," Leila said, putting a pretend scowl on her face and shaking her head. "After all, what are the chances of her being wrong?"

"And why do we call her Julietta, anyway?" Lizzy asked. "We always have, but it's so long. Never Julie, never Jules. Always Ju-li-et-ta."

"It's a pretty name," Leila said.

"It is at that," Lizzy said, turning her head to the left to look outside, "but I still wonder. It's just so formal."

"But you know," Mary said, starting to relax, "I had a friend in high school who everybody called Lawrence, never Larry, and a friend from even farther back who everybody called Andrew, never Andy."

"Or Drew," Lizzy said.

"I like that name," Leila said, and stretched her arms.

Then Mary looked sober again. "She never called me."

"What does she need to call *you* for?" Lizzy asked, wrinkling her brow and turning back to face Mary. "I'm the one who was supposed to drive her here."

Leila laughed. "You'll see her soon enough and then you'll realize you were missing her for nothing."

"I think she's jealous of you," Lizzy said, crossing her legs and raising her eyebrows.

"Why should she be jealous of me?" Mary asked, but she was still looking at Leila.

Mary expected Lizzy to say, "Because you're famous, or are about to be," but Lizzy said, "You don't react to things the way she does. Not everything strikes you as an emergency."

Leila laughed. "Or a calamity. Or a catastrophe."

"She wishes she had your ability to shrug things off," Lizzy said emphatically, leaning forward.

And Mary wondered, What makes her think I can shrug anything off? Maybe, she thought, she was less honest with people than she realized.

Then Mary stood up and said, "Leila, let me ask you a question. Do you feel anything where you're sitting?"

"Feel anything?" Leila asked. She ran her hands horizontally along the cushion she was sitting on, looking first to her left, then to her right, and said, "No. Nothing. Should I?"

Mary looked relieved. "No, I was just curious." She then expected Leila or Lizzy to say "Something is definitely wrong," but neither one did. "So where are we eating?" she asked, sounding happy in a put-on way.

"I'm glad you asked," Leila said, and smiled again. Sometimes her perfect teeth bothered Mary. Too big. They made her smile seem insincere. "Susan Elizabeth's Tea Room."

"Oh, that sounds nice," Mary said.

"Have you ever been there?" Lizzy asked.

"I haven't."

"Which might be why it sounds nice," Leila said.

But familiarity is what always sounded nice to Mary, not something new. Leila should have known that. Though if you don't expose yourself to people, you can't criticize them for not understanding you.

"And where is Julietta meeting us?" Mary asked.

"At the restaurant," Lizzy said.

"At the restaurant? But she's not eating there."

"When we're done," Leila said. "Outside. It won't be awkward."

For a moment Mary thought of asking them if they'd like to hear her play something, but she didn't bother, because neither Leila nor Lizzy had the slightest interest in classical music, and Mary figured they'd just be bored. You can communicate to an audience, but the audience has to want to hear what you're playing.

"Come," Leila said, getting up, stretching, and, after thinking about it for a moment, yawning. "Let's go."

They walked into town along Shore Road, which was, even up there, bereft of traffic, but as they got farther down, Mary became uncomfortable. She wasn't sure why, but she didn't like crowds. Audiences, of course, were different. An audience pays money to see you. In a crowd you were just a stranger and, ultimately, you didn't matter. You would be ignored until and unless you did something that brought attention to yourself, and then, after a moment, you would be ignored again.

Susan Elizabeth's Tea Room was on Shore Road, just two blocks down from Lampert Street, where the Pànduàn Room was, which meant it was one block north of Coralis Avenue, which was already thick with crowds. You could hear Rhoda and her musical friends pretty much wherever you walked, but if your mind was occupied by something else, it became background noise like the hum of a refrigerator that you'd notice only when it stopped. On the main streets a lot of people were browsing through the racks of clothes that the clothing stores had moved onto the sidewalk, and tables were covered with wares that various vendors were looking to sell. In front of Deb and Guy's Bake Shop, cloth-covered folding tables were laid out with handcrafted—to use a term of the day—donuts, pies, macarons, and, of course, their famous vanilla cupcakes, all covered in glass cloches to keep out the heat and insects. No one could smell anything, but that would bring visitors inside, where it was comfortably cool and they could relish the aromas of fresh-baked goods. In front of JC's Salon, an art gallery with a glass-enclosed porch, paintings, mostly modern, or "contemporary," as Mel would say, and prints, some elaborately framed, some very simply framed, were set up on easels, along with a small round table holding complementary glasses of white wine. Across the street, at the only triangle in town, where Garrett's Alley and Eli Nam Street both ended at Shore Road, was Callaghan's Restaurant—not a pub—and there six tables with patio umbrellas were already full, with many more people waiting to be seated. Across Cope Street was Terzino's Italian Ices, where Pete Terzino, the owner, who had originally wanted to name his establishment Petey's, a pun on both his given name and his initials, set out freezers containing his specialties, pistachio ices, chocolate ices, and piña colada ices, along with more familiar fare, and then they passed Suzie's Animal Shelter, where a mass of people were already looking at homeless dogs and cats, who would be rolled inside after about ten minutes in the sun, to give another half-dozen pets their chance to find a forever home and keep the first group of pets cool. Really the only establishments that didn't offer anything were the three churches, Catholic, Presbyterian, and Lutheran; the bank; the dry cleaner; the Masonic Temple; Capricorn's Barber Shop; and the law offices of LeGronk, Anduze, and Henry, but that, at least, let people's imaginations wander.

When they got to Susan Elizabeth's, the first thing Mary heard was Leila shout, "Well look who's here!" Mary looked up, and there was Julietta, standing straight and tall, as she invariably would, but, of course, not smiling. She had a very high forehead, long black hair that was combed back, and a protrusive brow, beneath which her face seemed to recede. It was narrow and held large, dark brown eyes and a small mouth. If only, Mary thought, less would come out of that mouth than usual. Julietta looked sad and a little annoyed and, shaking her head, she said, "I got done with my work early, so I figured I'd meet you guys here. I thought I'd surprise you."

"Where did you park?" Leila asked.

"At Mary's house. I hope that's all right."

"Of course," Mary said. She looked around and saw a dozen people lined up to get into the restaurant. "Did anybody make a reservation, perhaps?"

"I did," Leila said. "They said we can go right in."

"So it's going to be four now, rather than three," Mary said.

"Does that bother you?" Julietta asked.

Of course it does, Mary thought, but she didn't say anything.

They were seated at a round ebony table—all of the tables there were round; none was square or rectangular—set with lace placemats and, in the center, a single yellow rose in a narrow vase, next to a candle on a short brass candlestick. "I love the smell of burnt flowers," Julietta said. She sat across from Lizzy, and Leila sat across from Mary. An elderly woman with curly gray hair and a baggy face, who was smartly attired in a short coral dress and pearls, handed them menus and said, "Take your time. And please understand than any of our hot teas can be served iced, which I would recommend on a day like this." Then she walked away.

The walls were covered in striped paper alternating indigo and bone, with off-white wainscoting beneath. Understated elegance, Mary thought, though the place was so cold and dim that she though the air conditioning must have used up whatever power kept the place lit. She thought back to her father and his friend Carmelo, whom he knew when he was growing up, and whom he loved to talk about. Carmelo had lived in a small house that had only one air conditioner—this was long before the days of central air—and that air conditioner was in the master bedroom. On summer nights, when Vim would occasionally sleep over, Carmelo's parents would set up a cot for Carmelo and, when appropriate, a sleeping bag for Vim, to sleep next to their bed, so they could all be comfortable. Of course the bedroom door had to be kept closed, but walking from a hot, stuffy hallway into a room that was maybe twenty degrees cooler was both shocking and, to Carmelo and Vim, delightful. Mary wondered about the loss that often comes with having too much.

"What is everyone eating?" Leila asked.

"I don't know," Julietta said. "I haven't looked at my menu yet."

It's printed on one page, Mary thought. How long is it going to take?

Leila ordered an English cucumber and cream cheese sandwich on white bread, Lizzy ordered smoked Scottish salmon and ground mustard on pumpernickel, Mary ordered chicken pot pie, because she knew she wouldn't be eating a big dinner that night, and Julietta ordered arugula salad with sliced Fuji apples, bacon, and brie in a raspberry vinaigrette. All of them had the soup of the day, which was, appropriately, crab bisque, and everyone but Mary ordered iced peach tea. Mary ordered iced oolong tea, which she thought tasted like peaches.

"So you've been here before," Mary said once the food came.

Leila glanced around the table. *Should I tell her?* "Yes, last year when we went to see Shelley."

"You went to see Shelley?"

Leila took a bite of her sandwich and nodded.

"You know we did," Lizzy said quietly. "We asked you if you wanted to come and you said no."

"Well you could have called me or come over," Mary said, resting her right palm just beneath her throat.

Julietta shook her head. "No we couldn't, and you know that. You don't like unexpected visitors. At least that's what you told us."

Leila swallowed. "Unless it's just us she doesn't like seeing unexpectedly."

Mary leaned back. "No, Julietta is right. I'd rather not."

"That's fine," Leila said, kicking Mary's feet under the table and giggling.

"That's why you could never throw a good party," Julietta said. "You separate people. Your different friends don't mingle with each other."

Mary didn't have any other friends, but thought it was nice that the friends she did have believed she had more.

"So tell me about the book you're working on," Lizzy said, looking at Julietta.

She laughed and bowed her head, as though laughing were something to be ashamed of. "That's why I was late today," Julietta said. "I'm having a problem with the author. Or, rather, he's having a problem with me." She took several bites of her salad and several spoonfuls of soup, though it was obvious to everyone that she wanted them to ask questions.

"What kind of problem?" Leila asked, looking genuinely concerned. Mary was impressed, She never could have looked that interested.

Julietta swallowed and shrugged. "What kind of problem does an artist ever have with an author? I'm finished with the book, or nearly finished, having drawn more than fifty...well, okay, forty pictures for it, and having shown him everything, and now he decides he doesn't like it. He doesn't think my drawings capture the essence of what he's trying to say."

"But he's still going to pay you for it, isn't he?" Lizzy asked.

"He is," Julietta said, without changing her expression, but moving her right arm forward, "but that isn't the point. The point is that now he wants to pull the job and find another artist, and that hurts."

"I can understand that," Mary said, nibbling at her pot pie and eating her soup with it.

"No, you can't understand it," Julietta said, "because you don't know why it hurts. It hurts because...well, if he'd told me, after I'd done one drawing, that what I was doing was no good, I could have changed it." She sipped her tea.

"But...," Lizzy said.

"But you wasted your time on thirty-nine more drawings," Mary said, still trying to sound supportive.

"No!" Julietta said. "That's not the point." Again. Mary shook her head. "The point is that after one picture he'd just be telling me that I fucked up once, but after forty, he's telling me—," Julietta realized she was talking too loudly, so she lowered her voice, "I'm being rejected forty times."

Mary turned away. "That's one way of looking at it," she said. She refolded the napkin in her lap.

"No," Julietta said, "that's the only way of looking at it."

Mary, whose own way of getting through life could be criticized for a certain narrowness, hated it when other people told her there was only one way to do something. Again, possibly because she did the same thing but didn't want to admit it to herself. Though here things were different. Mary's "narrowness" at least made her happy, but Julietta's narrowness seemed to leave her in perpetual despair. Then Mary realized why she'd been so anxious about Julietta not being at her house earlier. She'd always seen Julietta as something to endure, and once that stretch of endurance was over, she could be forgotten. Walked away from. The anticipation was worse than the reality. Usually.

"What kind of book is it?" Lizzy asked.

And again Julietta laughed. Was it because Mary hadn't asked the question? "It's called *Key, the Alligator*."

"What kind of title is that?" Mary asked, picking at the vegetables she still hadn't eaten.

"Everything okay?" the waitress asked, walking over quietly, bending between Mary and Julietta, and smiling. She was wearing too much perfume.

"Fine, thank you," Lizzy said.

"It's a story about an alligator that swallows people's keys." Julietta sighed. "You know how insane you get when you can't find your keys?

Well, this could be why. At least according to the book, which I now think was written by an idiot."

"What is it, an allegory?" Mary asked.

Julietta scrunched her face. "No, of course not. It's a *children*'s book. And in the course of the story, as people lose their keys, they realize that their pet alligator—"

Mary laughed. "Oh, he's a *pet*."

"Yes," Julietta said, as though to emphasize how important that point was. "And he swallows this family's keys, and when that happens they realize they can't unlock things anymore, or go anywhere, because, well, they can't get into their car, they can't get into their house if they find themselves on the outside—"

"Are you sure this isn't an allegory? Because I'm sure somebody could draw, *no pun intended*, a lot of insights into human nature from what you're telling me."

"You're overthinking it," Julietta said flatly, and looked defensive.

"The life unexamined is not worth living," Mary said. "Socrates."

Julietta turned to Mary. "Is *your* life worth living? Julietta Han."

For a few moments nobody spoke. Then Leila said, "She was kidding," lightly kicking Mary's feet again.

"You know," Mary said, "I used to think you were the kind of person who walks around with a black cloud over her head. But you're not. You're the black cloud that sits over everyone else's head, because you find fault with others that you can't find with yourself."

"*You* never find fault with yourself," Julietta said.

And Mary thought, You have no idea.

Then, after a few more silent moments, Lizzy took a deep breath and said, "Could you imagine him trying to get through airport security? With all that metal in him? Key, I mean. Key, the alligator."

"Not to mention the fact that, I'm assuming, he'd have to stay wet," Leila said.

"Alligators can sit out of water," Mary said.

"Not if he was flying. No flight is short enough. And you know, since

9/11, you're limited on how much liquid you can carry onto a plane."

"They're like crabs, I think," Leila said, but she sounded uninterested. "Come. Let's get out of here."

And that was why Mary never enjoyed being with her friends. One at a time was okay, but all three of them together depressed her, because there was always tension, and she didn't know why.

Slowly they walked to the intersection of Shore Road and Coralis Avenue. It was packed with people, and Rhoda was singing with her musical friends, who were playing their hearts out. Or so it seemed.

"What happens if it rains?" Mary asked.

"They put a tent over the proceedings," Leila said. "Now, you see how the whole intersection is roped off? That's because you have to buy a ticket to see Shelley. Then you can get inside. You can hear the band"—it wasn't a band—"and the singer just fine, but you can't watch Shelley dance. Because the tank she's in"—it wasn't a tank—"isn't clear. Clever, right?"

"This town needs a boardwalk," Lizzy said.

"No, it doesn't," Julietta said. "It would attract the wrong kind of people."

"Listen to you!" Leila said. "Who are 'the wrong kind of people'?"

"I don't know," Julietta said, and shrugged. "People who cause trouble."

"She's just jealous because Onica Lake doesn't have a boardwalk, either," Lizzy said.

"Boardwalks are fun," Leila said. "They're nice for strolling, and most of the people they attract, in fact, almost all of them, are perfectly fine."

Mary was waiting for one of them to say that Julietta was starting to sound like her, but neither did.

"Oh, you know what I read?" Leila asked. "They want to open a restaurant here called The 5 E's. Now what do you think of when you hear '5 E's'?"

"Extremely wide shoes," Mary said.

"Exactly. But the owners are naming it for their children: Edward, Emily, Edna, Elinor, and Elisma."

"Elisma?" Lizzy asked.

"That's what I read," Leila said. "Unless it was a misprint."

Mary hated the cuteness and disrespect of giving all of one's children

190 ERIC J. MATLUCK

names that started with the same letter. It erased their individuality and made them seem like variants of one another.

"Well, something new is always good," Lizzy said.

"Not in this town," Mary said. "You know what happens here? Nobody wants change, so things change not so much gradually as strategically. Listen, I'm not making this up. Every two or three years a launderette that had been converted into a hardware store is converted back into a launderette, or a new Italian restaurant opens around the corner from an old Italian restaurant that just closed down. So people never have to wait long to recapture the illusion of stasis. That's what they want."

"Maybe," Leila said thoughtfully.

"You don't live here, so you don't know," Mary said, "but I do."

They got to the intersection of Shore Road and Coralis Avenue, and nearly a hundred people were standing at the street corners and on the crosswalks. Maybe half as many had paid to get inside the area that was roped off.

"How much are the tickets?" Mary asked.

"Fifty cents," Leila said.

"Fifty cents?" Lizzy asked. "What costs fifty cents anymore? Do they still make quarters?

Mary reached into her right skirt pocket and pulled out a handful of change that included four quarters. "Yeah, they do."

"Well look at the dates," Lizzy said. "I bet they're old."

They all laughed.

"And where can we buy them? The tickets, I mean," Mary asked.

"Over there," Leila said. She pointed to a small ticket booth that sat on the southeast corner of the intersection, which was on the left and across the street as they walked down Shore Road.

There were about twenty people standing on line, which was almost half the number of people who were standing within the roped-off section. Which meant that nobody was actually standing that close to Shelley for more than a minute or two, maybe because the music was too loud or maybe because there wasn't much to see. To Mary, it was starting to feel late already. "I'll buy them then," she said. "Four." She crossed Shore Road, then Coralis Avenue and, turning to look back at her friends, she walked into somebody who was already standing on line but who had taken a few steps backward, himself. "Oh, I'm sorry," she said, then turned back to look at Leila, Lizzy, and Julietta. They'd already crossed Shore Road and were walking toward her. When she would later describe the incident to people, she would say that walking into the man was actually strangely comforting, because it felt like walking into a giant stuffed animal, or, she might have said, like wrapping herself in her down comforter.

But that was odd, because the man was tall, about six-foot-three, lean, muscular, and very unforgiving. He was wearing a white t-shirt, a pair of neatly pressed blue jeans, and a pair of white high tops. He was in his early twenties, had close-cropped blond hair, bright blue eyes, unusually long eyelashes, a thin, straight nose, and a mouth so perfectly horizontal that it could have been drawn by a draftsman. His skin was pale. He raised his hands as though, bear-like, he were about to attack her, but suddenly stopped when, Mary thought, he saw that she was a woman, and started to laugh. "Oh, sweet Jesus," he said. "It's a Jaundy girl."

Leila, Lizzy, and Julietta had just walked up behind Mary and heard what the man said. Of the four, Leila was the only one who was familiar with the expression, having been called that before, but the others could figure out what it meant. It was a reference to Mary's yellow and, as he saw it, *jaundiced* skin. Mary recalled the first judge having mentioned that, and her heart sank, but she never perceived the judges as a threat. She was less sure about the man.

"And look," he said. "There's fucking more. They must breed like rabbits. The way those other people do." Mary knew he was referring to Blacks, and hated the fact that she knew that.

Just then a girl of seventeen, identically dressed, but short and stocky, much less pale, with a heart-shaped face, a pouty expression, thick lips, and darker blonde hair that she wore in cornrows, walked up to the man and stood next to him. She was coming from the opposite direction as Leila, Lizzy, and Julietta. "What's going on here?" she asked. Her voice was strikingly deep, almost masculine.

"What's going on?" the man asked, still smiling but not turning to look at her. "This gook bitch fucking walked into me. And she didn't even say 'I'm sorry.'"

The girl looked at Mary and shook her head. "Don't pay any attention to him," she said. "He's not from around here."

And Mary wondered what that meant. Neither the man nor the teenage girl spoke with an accent, but, of course, "not from around here" could have meant "from the next town over." Still, to Mary, he was the foreigner, not her.

The girl rolled her eyes, slapped him on the top of his left arm, and said, "Leave her alone. Let's go."

"No," he said with exaggerated patience. "I don't want to go. I want to have some fun first. I want this slant cunt to know what she did."

The words were familiar; Ken had called her all of that, but she could forgive him, and then she wondered why. Maybe she shouldn't have. Maybe it was never okay to speak to someone like that, no matter how familiar or comfortable you felt with them. Mary's heart was pounding, yet she could have sworn she was watching herself, the man, and the teenage girl from a distance.

The man clenched his right fist. "You didn't watch where you were going," he said, trying to sound angrier than he was.

"I—," Mary said, about to remind him that she'd already said she was sorry, but instead stood in front of him, staring.

"But you couldn't. You couldn't see me because you can't open those goddamned broken eyes!"

And Mary was devastated. Nobody had to explain to her what he meant. She knew what her eyes looked like; she'd known all her life. She thought they were beautiful...

"They look like two broken globes with cracks in them."

...But maybe, she thought, she shouldn't. Maybe they weren't beautiful.

Leila, Lizzy, and Julietta took a few steps back, but none was going to leave, though none said anything, either. But then, neither did anyone else. Absolutely nobody around them said anything or even paid attention to what was going on. They all had their own lives to lead.

Mary imagined seeing Jesse in the crowd, and him telling the man, who was about Jesse's age, that he or, even better, his older brother, was going to beat the shit out of him. But she dismissed that as a childish fantasy, and didn't stop to consider why she'd had it. Whether it was because she was so scared or because she liked Jesse more than she realized. Then she thought about Ken, and convinced herself, because she had to, that he would stand up for her. He might have called her the same things, but he could get away with it. But again, no, she thought, he couldn't. She didn't care that he was family and she didn't care what the judges thought. He was wrong.

"You people made us all sick," the man said. He was referring to COVID. "You still make me sick."

How did he know I'm Chinese? Mary wondered. Unless he just groups all Asians together. The next thing he's going to do is blame us for Pearl Harbor. Without meaning to, she laughed.

And that, not surprisingly, got the man angrier. "Look at that!" he said, pointing his right index finger at her. "The cunt is laughing at me. She's making fun of me. What would happen if I slit your ugly throat?!" he yelled.

And again she thought about her brother, then more compassionately, because he would never strike her and would never threaten anyone with bodily harm. Then Mary started crying. "I'd bleed," she said. But after that, whether out of disgust with Ken, disgust with the man, disgust with the fact that absolutely nobody was turning his or her fucking head to look, she yelled out, "You can't! You can't slit my ugly throat. Because it's not ugly!" Which surprised her at least as much as it surprised him.

She wondered then if she was dreaming, or if the judges had arranged the encounter, but no, as soon as she'd wonder about a dream, she'd wake up, and the judges had already explained that they didn't have the power to create people for her.

Was that Pete Terzino she saw walking up? He'd run the man out of town, she thought, but she thought that because he was Italian, so of a minority, too, and she needed to stop thinking that way, believing that because he might have felt put-upon, he would defend anyone else who felt put-upon.

The teenage girl next to the man punched him twice on his left arm and said, "Leave her the fuck alone!" Mary believed she was serious.

"God made this country for White men!" he said. "And we're taking it back! Do you hear me?! We're fucking taking it back!"

The teenage girl clicked her tongue and said, "She's not deaf. Leave her alone!"

Mary couldn't understand why the girl seemed to be defending her. At first she thought it was because both she and Mary were female, but then she decided, or perhaps realized, that the girl was simply getting tired of the whole thing. Mary was only thinking the way she'd thought before, that all oppressed people help all other oppressed people. They don't. And not everyone felt oppressed.

"God must have been struck blind when he made gooks," the man said, and laughed, evidently delighted with his own inventiveness.

And Mary thought about that. God. Of course, you had to mention God, to show you were a man of principle and conviction, a true believer. Easier, that way, to convince yourself that you, like God, were always right and everybody else was wrong. But what did he mean by "struck blind"? That God had struck himself blind after he'd created the Chinese people, because it was such a mistake, or that God had a moment of impure vision, during which the Chinese people were, no doubt mistakenly, created?

Then she realized that since the whole altercation started, neither one of them had moved. But neither had Leila, Lizzy, or Julietta. The whole scene might have been manipulated by a puppeteer who didn't have enough dexterity to bring his characters to life.

"Come on; leave her alone," the teenage girl said, and turned away.

"Why?" the man asked. "What am I afraid of? That she's going to hold it against me?" He sniffed and smiled. "Don't worry. Animals are forgiving."

And Mary, who thought the best thing she could do was walk away before the man turned violent, decided to stand right where she was and stare at him. Not because she was afraid he would follow her or afraid she'd look weak to whoever was paying attention—and she really didn't think anybody was—but because she knew that if she did walk away, his imagined taunts would obsess her. The taunts he hadn't made, but that she expected him to make. She knew that those would be far more damaging, because she understood her insecurities and vulnerabilities better than he did. Nobody could hurt her as cleanly and efficiently as she could hurt herself.

She thought then, not unexpectedly and even necessarily, about something she loved; her music. She understood that there would always be people at her recitals who didn't respond the way she hoped they would, but their lives weren't her life and different things moved, impressed, and satisfied them, just as different things moved, impressed, and satisfied this man. Did she need to know what they were? No. It was over. Another missed connection. Just someone else she didn't please. Now these were certainly not the same thing, giving a recital and receiving verbal abuse, but we try to explain the unfamiliar in terms of the known even if, at times, such comparisons breed prejudice.

And then, less than a minute later, the man cleared his throat, made a sound like he was about to spit at her, but instead shook the middle finger of his right hand, swallowed his saliva loudly, and said, "You have no idea how lucky you are." Then he turned to the woman and said, "You kick shit and all you do is get your shoes dirty. Let's get the fuck out of here. I'm not going to stand on line with a goddamned chink." And then they walked away.

Mary wanted to say, That's right, get out of here. Get out, you bore me. You *bore* me. But she didn't, because she was afraid. Still afraid. And she hated herself for being afraid. Until she finally realized that she was right. He did bore her. Bored her at least as much as he'd frightened her. And because of that, she didn't need to say anything. He was just a man without a name, someone entirely not worth talking to, someone entirely not worth listening to, and someone entirely not worth trying to understand. He didn't matter.

INTERVIEWER: You must have enjoyed the reception you got at the end of last night's performance.

MARY (*Laughs*): Of course I did. But to a point. Only to a point.

INTERVIEWER: To a point? To what point?

MARY: It was nice, of course, but sometimes it's a hit and sometimes it's a miss, and that's all part of the game. Hits, of course, are better than misses, but not as much as you might think.

INTERVIEWER: Why?

MARY: Because when you're a hit you receive adulation, and adulation is like sex.

INTERVIEWER: Excuse me?!

MARY (*Almost reprimanding*): Come on, we're mature adults. I can talk about it openly and you know exactly what I mean. You work hard at a performance; playing a piano is not like playing jacks. It takes physical, emotional, and mental endurance, stamina, and effort. And when you're done, and the audience *explodes* in applause, if they do, it's like ejaculation. (*Laughs*) Theirs, of course, not mine. But then it's over and, as with sex, the feeling of euphoria, or whatever you want to call it, disappears quickly. Look, I know how to make myself happy but also, maybe more importantly, how to *keep* myself happy. Adulation doesn't *keep* me happy. It makes me happy for a time, but then it's gone.

INTERVIEWER: So you don't care if you don't please the audience.

MARY (*Disgusted*): Haven't we been through this before? Are you going to ask me the same goddamned questions until you get the answer you want? I care that I please myself. There are some people I'm not going to please, and, to be brutally honest, I can't waste my time trying.

Once everything unfroze and started moving again, Mary turned around, continued waiting in line until it was her turn to buy tickets, purchased four, thanked the man who sold them to her, then looked at her friends, her silent friends, who were standing right behind her. "Shut up," she said to Leila, as she handed her a ticket, "shut up," she said to Lizzy, as she handed her a ticket, "and shut up," she said to Julietta, as she handed her a ticket. "We came to see Shelley the Dancing Crab and that's what we're going to do. We'll talk when we get back to my house. If you don't want to talk, that's fine. You know where your cars are." Mary wasn't mad at them. She would have done the same thing they did if she were in their position; kept quiet. And she wasn't being manipulative, or wasn't trying to be. She just didn't want to talk. She wanted and needed time to think, and she couldn't do that if people were chattering around her.

"But—," Julietta said.

And Lizzy shook her head. "He's gone. He didn't buy a ticket."

"That's not what he came for," Leila said, not smiling.

When they entered the roped-off area, where one could get close to the tub that held Shelley, Rhoda was singing *It Ain't Necessarily So*, and the musicians were, in fact, playing too loudly. The four friends watched the two men who were holding the tub on opposite sides shake it, and watched Shelley as she drifted back and forth in the water. The song lasted only four minutes, and Mary loved it, but as soon as it was over she crawled beneath the rope, looked behind her to make sure her friends were following, and they all sauntered silently back to her house.

In the living room, Mary sat on the piano bench, Leila sat on the left side of the couch, so on top of the first judge, Julietta sat on the right side of the couch, so on top of the third judge, and Lizzy sat in the recliner.

"He was an asshole," Lizzy said.

Mary smiled and asked her friends if they wanted anything to drink.

"Nothing for me, thanks," Leila said. "I've got to get going soon. What time is it?"

Mary wondered why she was asking that. She was wearing a watch. But Leila wanted everyone to know that she wasn't going to stay much longer, and simply looking at her watch wouldn't have made that as obvious.

Julietta, frowning, held her left wrist in front of her. "Three forty-eight," she said.

"How anal," Mary said. "Can't you say 'almost ten to four'?"

"I'm wearing a digital watch," Julietta said.

"They still make those?" Mary asked.

Leila laughed and shook her head. "You know, you really are unaware of the world around you. Yes, *they still make those.*"

"That's why you love me," Mary said, throwing her head back. "It's part of who I am. You have to take the whole package."

"That's right," Leila said. "No 'one from column A and two from column B.'"

But Mary's smile fell; she found that degrading and unfunny.

Lizzy leaned forward. "Okay," she said calmly. Then, "So Jesus Christ, Mary; what did you just stand there for? He could have killed you."

"Oh, we're back to that?" Mary asked. "Because he didn't matter," she said. Perhaps she'd become inured to such abuse through Ken.

"He didn't, but you do," Lizzy said. "I don't understand you."

"You don't have to," Mary said disinterestedly.

"I would have called the police," Lizzy said.

Mary turned to her and said, "You were there, too. Why didn't you? You were in a better position to do that than I was." And when Lizzy opened her mouth to speak, Mary said dryly, "It doesn't matter, and I'm not berating you for it. You're just saying that now because the damage is done." She thought back to the night her mother died. She was sitting in the waiting room on the fourth floor of Thomas Jefferson University Hospital in Philadelphia, with her Aunt Clara, her mother's older sister, and when the nurse came to tell them that Margaret had passed, Clara said to Mary, "I would sue the doctor who let this happen." Ken wasn't there, of course, because he didn't like the Chinese side of the family. "If you were so concerned," Mary said, "you should have looked for the police while he was harassing me."

Lizzy looked embarrassed, then said, "You looked like you didn't care."

Then Mary shook her head and said, "He was just someone else."

Lizzy wanted to, but decided not to criticize the distance Mary kept from others, so she said nothing. Leila and Julietta, who kept silent, too, had discussed it with her many times, then given up, but Lizzy had always been afraid to mention it, because she was White and Leila and Julietta were both Asian, and Lizzy didn't want to think that Mary was keeping a distance from her because she was different. Even if she knew that Mary kept a distance from everybody. So Lizzy's silence stemmed from fear, not respect or compassion, but, of course, Mary couldn't have known that and, just as of course, Mary couldn't have cared less.

Leila erupted in laughter. "I loved it when he said that God made this country for White men." She raised her right hand, then fluttered it, sneering. "Interesting that he didn't mention White women, because if God didn't make this country for them, too, White men won't be around much longer."

Nobody reacted, which disappointed Leila.

Lizzy leaned to her right. "People like him say they love God and country, but they don't. They can't love anybody. They don't know how."

Mary picked up her head and sat forward. "That's right; they don't. Love is something that needs to be learned. I think we're born with trust, but not with love."

Julietta sighed. "Some people aren't capable of love, are they, Mary?" She looked toward the piano.

"No, they aren't, *are they, Julietta*?" Her voice was raspy.

Leila waved her hands in front of her. "Come on, you guys; knock it off."

"Can I get anyone a drink?" Mary asked. She'd asked before and no one had wanted anything, but they all thought they'd be leaving shortly, and by the second time Mary asked, they thought they weren't.

"Do you have iced tea?" Leila asked.

"I do. Freshly made. Not freshly brewed, but close enough," Mary said.

"I'll take one, please," Leila said.

"Me, too," Lizzy said.

"I'll pass," Julietta said.

Of course, Mary thought. A few minutes later, she came back with three tall glasses filled to the rim, and the atmosphere seemed to have softened.

"It wasn't anything personal," Julietta said, looking more lachrymose than usual.

Expressionlessly, Mary said, "I understand."

"Look," Julietta said, "it's hard being a member of a minority."

But Mary shook her head and said dourly, "Oh, bullshit, Julietta. It comes naturally enough to me."

INTERVIEWER: How does it feel to be an Indian/Asian woman?

MARY: I don't know, because I've never been anything else. And you can say "Chinese" rather than "Asian." Might as well be specific and not lump me with everybody else; we're not all the same. And when you say "Indian," meaning someone from India, or whose relatives are from India, say "Asian Indian" so people don't think you're talking about Native Americans. Jesus Christ, what year is it? Don't you know that yet? You decided, or were assigned, to interview me. Know who the hell you're talking to.

Julietta had once dated a man who playfully, lovingly, or whatever rationale he wanted to use, called her "Bop," because she was Korean and "bop" was the Korean word for rice. At first she thought it was cute, but then realized that when a man said he was "dating brown rice," it meant he was dating someone Asian, and the term could have other, less savory, connotations. In the long run she broke up with him.

And that, Mary thought, was why she kept getting together with her friends every so often. But only every so often. Because she didn't enjoy their company. If she really wanted to, or maybe if she were smart, she would simply stop seeing them. But what drove her was the possibility that the next time they got together, she would have a reasonably good time. The way she'd had with her friends from high school that one Thanksgiving weekend, her first semester in college. The weekend that couldn't be repeated, but that she could always relive whenever she listened to Brahms' First Violin Sonata. So if she could have that good a time with Leila, Lizzy, and Julietta, just once, she'd never have to see them again, but could remember them fondly, or more than fondly, whenever she listened to something else. She decided then that she would listen to that old recording of the Brahms that night, and that made her happy. It gave her something to look forward to. Which made being with Leila, Lizzy, and Julietta a little easier to put up with. Maybe she'd just outgrown them, she thought. Or maybe she'd never grown into them to begin with.

"I bet that man was abused," Lizzy said. "Maybe as a child."

"Life is abusive," Mary said.

"Maybe he just wanted to be famous once," Leila said, lifting her eyebrows.

"And then he was forgotten," Mary said.

"You know what I used to do at my first job?" Lizzy asked.

"Can't wait to hear this," Julietta said.

Lizzy smiled. "No, it's really funny. Or at least I think it is."

"Which means it's not," Julietta said.

"I used to make up names for the people I worked with. Alternate names. You know how you give people nicknames?" She leaned back and started gesticulating with her hands. "People do it all the time. With friends, loved ones, children. But I went a little farther. I gave each of my coworkers a first name and a last name."

Leila looked at her dumbly. "Why?!"

Lizzy shrugged. "I thought it would be fun."

"Sounds awfully controlling to me," Leila said.

"Talk about not accepting people for who they are, only for who you want them to be," Mary said.

"Yes," Lizzy said, "right, but you're born with a name and, unless you change it, and most people don't, it usually doesn't say much about you. I mean, how many people named Cooper are barrel-makers? So I picked names that could subtly describe people."

Leila shook her head and rolled her eyes. "That must have made you popular."

"Give us an example," Mary said, hoping that Lizzy would understand that "an" meant "one."

"Okay, I used to work with this Jewish guy named Aaron Kroll. And I'll tell you in a moment why I mentioned that he was Jewish. Aaron—I loved that man—was sweet, super-intelligent, very good-looking, but oh my God, he was such a slob. So I named him Irving Kesselman. Do you get it? *Irving*, because I wanted to give him a Jewish name," Mary and Leila groaned, "and *Kesselman* as a pun on *Kesselgarden*, which was a Yiddishism for 'mess.' Don't ask me why."

Leila laughed too loudly. "Oh, don't worry," she said. "We won't."

"What's the point of all of this?" Mary asked.

"So that guy who threatened you today. I thought we should give him a name so, you know, if you want to—"

And Leila, uncharacteristically, yelled "No! No, no, no! Lizzy, look, I know you're not a moron, but that has got to be the most stupid thing you've ever said. He's gone, dead, buried. Let it go."

And Mary thought, Gone, dead, buried. Maybe she should call him Ben. Then she laughed, thinking about what she'd just heard. Maybe he *did* want to be famous once. Because people who were famous *once* always end up gone, dead, and buried. And often forgotten. No, the name Ben would remind her of only one person she knew.

Leila again looked at her watch, but that time said, "Look, it's time to go."

"Yes, it is," Lizzy said quietly. Mary wasn't sure whether Lizzy wanted to stay, but didn't think she did. Both of them got up.

Julietta shook her head. "I don't need to go," she said, "unless you want me to."

And Mary didn't know how to answer that, because Julietta took most forms of goodbye as a request that she leave. But Mary said, "That's up to you," which, effectively, put the responsibility on Julietta's shoulders.

"I'll go," Julietta said noncommittally, but Mary knew they would both be happier. That said, when Mary spent time with Julietta alone, she found her much less critical and less dismal than when all four of them got together. Julietta didn't feel comfortable with more than one person at a time, and when she felt threatened, as she must have by three people, her defenses would be sharpened.

A few minutes after her friends were gone, and Mary stood by the kitchen window, watching them pull away, without waving, just as she'd watched them pull up, she made herself a salad of romaine lettuce, sliced cucumber, sliced radish, feta cheese, black olives, and a lemon vinaigrette, and poured herself a glass of tomato juice, but after taking two bites of the salad and thinking she wasn't hungry, then taking a third bite and realizing she was correct, she brought it over to the counter, wrapped it in plastic, and put it in the refrigerator. For later, she thought. Or maybe tomorrow.

She took the glass of tomato juice to her bedroom and lay down on her bed without unmaking it. It was much too early to get under the covers, and she was sure the judges would have something to say about what happened that afternoon, whether it was about her interaction with the man whom she wouldn't name, so who, as far as she was concerned, had no name, or about her interaction with her friends. She laughed, thinking it might not be so bad if the judges decided unfavorably, because just then she couldn't imagine wanting to see Leila, Lizzy, or Julietta any time soon, and if she'd been removed from the nameless man's memory, she might be better off.

Then she thought about that, took a sip of tomato juice, and realized she wouldn't be. She didn't deserve to be forgotten; he did. And then she laughed, thinking that maybe he had his own panel of judges—he must have!—who would come to their own "negative" opinion about him, and she'd forget him until he did something to reverse that. And that, she knew, would be a long time.

But she couldn't get him out of her mind. One thing that scared her so much was his use of the word "broken." Not because she didn't want to think of herself, or any part of her, as broken, but because she'd never heard it used that way. She thought that all prejudiced, bigoted people were stupid, misinformed, and unenlightened. They didn't know how to express themselves. Well, that was what she got for not exposing herself more openly to prejudice. Or just learning how to ignore it. Cleverness, if you could call it that, was never a quality she'd attributed to them, but clever people, rather than stupid people, were ultimately more dangerous, because they could think of more effective ways to cause trouble. Maybe it wasn't ignorance people should be afraid of; maybe it was cunning.

And then she thought he might have been right. Maybe she *was* broken. Yes, agreeing with someone for the sake of agreement was always the easiest way of ending an argument, and she knew she was arguing with herself, but if he hadn't told her something that was true, she could have walked away unbothered, right? The things that made her happy weren't the things that made most people happy, so why should they make *her* happy? Maybe being happy was the wrong thing to do, maybe being happy was the wrong way to feel. She sipped her juice. The fact was this: more people hated the things that the nameless man hated than loved the things that she loved.

She turned over on her left side and looked at the lamp on her nightstand. Simple and plain. She never minded being depressed or hurt if she could learn from it. Then something occurred to her. She'd spent her entire life tearing herself up in the exact same way the nameless man had. She knew that. Nobody ever asked her, "Why are you so *different*?" Nobody ever said, "You should like the things *we* like." Only Mary said that. To herself. And if you asked her why, as I once did, she would say, "I guess it's to inoculate myself. Against other people's disapproval, or what I perceive as other people's disapproval. If I could hurt myself enough by telling myself enough terrible things, other people's slings and arrows wouldn't bother me. I'd be numb." But that, she would then admit, was a horrible, though unfortunately common, way to go through life, and those thoughts never took hold for very long. Was she broken? Was she wrong? As long as she thought she was, she was standing in judgment of herself just the way the nameless man had, and that made her no better than him. Then she raised her head from the pillow, took a long swallow of tomato juice, and realized what she'd done. And Oh, my God, she thought. We're all judges.

That was when she understood, or thought she understood, who the three figures in her living room were, and why they couldn't show their faces. Because they would all look like her. When one had to repeatedly criticize oneself and constantly pass judgment, it became a chore, and to have someone else do it for her lightened the task. Was she right? Were the judges who she thought they were? She would find out only by asking them, but she was afraid to, because they might say no. They would never lie to her, she was sure of that, but she might have been wrong, and being wrong, in that instance, would have been devastating, because then they would have been strangers, not-quite-human or not-at-all-human entities that should have had no place in her home or her life but who wouldn't leave. She had to make her question subtle enough so their answer wouldn't ravage her. But if she was right, and they were mere extensions of her, they would have no more reason for being once she understood that, and then they would be gone.

She walked into the living room to practice. That was something she hadn't done in a few days. She had no recitals coming up soon, and she would often take a holiday weekend as an excuse to give her fingers and wrists a rest, but she loved playing. That night she played through *Lagniappe*, a nine-minute piano piece by Milton Babbitt, whose music Mary adored for its pervasive elegance. Yes, Babbitt had written computer-generated music, and most people found his works, computer-generated and otherwise, unlistenably barbed and edgy, but Mary never heard them that way. To her there was a refinement that called Mozart to mind, just Mozart transported to the Information Age.

INTERVIEWER: You told me before that you find much twentieth-century music "exquisite." How would you define "exquisite"?

MARY: Intricate. Elegant. Colorful. Refined. But mostly colorful, I think. In the way a Persian rug is exquisite. Or a piece of lace or an ice crystal, though there you have to appreciate the subtle gradations of color. Look, by the twentieth century instruments had reached a height of complexity and innovation that allowed them to be played in new ways, and that allowed them to produce new sounds and colors. Composers like Cage and Crumb found ways to play the piano that no one had ever thought of and, in so doing, introduced sounds that were, well, *exquisite*. But you don't have to "amplify" or "prepare" a piano to hear what I'm talking about. Debussy found more sheer color in the piano, played conventionally, than anyone had before him.

INTERVIEWER: You like color.

MARY (*Laughs*): I don't like white walls.

INTERVIEWER: Is that because you're not White?

MARY: White people aren't white. They're sort of a tannish-pink. I would paint my bathroom that color.

She played the piece once, got up, walked over to the drum table and looked outside, then played it differently a second time, then differently again twice more, highlighting alternative phrases each time, until, the fifth time she played it, it sounded right—pleasing and satisfying—to her. And as soon as she rested her hands in her lap, as she would at the end of a concert, she heard the whistle. She knew the judges would be passing judgment and she knew they would have to wait for her to finish doing what she was doing, now that she knew who they were. Maybe. So she turned around.

"Excellent, Mary," the first judge said.

"Very nice," the third judge said, nodding.

Mary looked embarrassed. "Do you always hear me practice?"

The second judge crossed his legs. "Of course we do. We hear everything. You ever go to sleep with a problem on your mind and suddenly wake up the next morning knowing how to solve it? That's because you're thinking even while you're asleep. It's the same thing with us. We don't move or talk or make noise—"

"Talk is often noise," the third judge said, and laughed.

"Of any kind, but we're aware of everything that goes on around us."

"You know why we're here, Mary," the first judge said gently.

"Don't worry," the second judge said, shaking his head. "It's all good."

And Mary covered her breast with her right hand and said, imitating surprise, "Oh, I'm sure it is." They have no control over me anymore, she thought.

Then the light in the brass lamp went out and Mary again saw the projection screen and slide projector, with the little felt cups around its feet, on the cocktail table.

"Then let's get started," the first judge said, leaning forward. "First slide, please."

And Mary saw Lizzy, Leila, and Julietta sitting at their table in Susan Elizabeth's Tea Room, having lunch. The fact that the image was seen from her point of view made Mary more certain that the judges were an extension of her.

"How often do you see your friends, Mary?" the first judge asked, first folding his arms across his chest then unfolding them.

Mary let her mouth drop and shook her head. "Not often. Maybe a few times a year."

"That's often enough," the second judge said. "Sometimes."

"Do you ever see them alone or do you always go out together?" the first judge asked.

Mary smiled vaguely. "We go out more together, to avoid hard feelings." And as she said that, she realized how odd the rationale was. "And you want to know something? Now that I think about it, I think it's ridiculous." Mary settled her blouse on her shoulders. "They're all jealous people. If I go out with one but not the others, the other two get offended and complain that we're leaving them out."

"Are your schedules so perfectly coordinated that you can always get together at the same time?" the first judge asked.

"That would be unusual," the third judge said, then cleared his throat.

"Well, Leila and Julietta are both freelancers, so their schedules are open. Lizzy, no, but we see each other mostly on weekends, and the occasional, make that *very* occasional, night out," Mary said.

"Do you prefer to see them as a group or individually?" the first judge asked.

"Always individually," Mary said.

The first judge leaned his head back so far that it faced the ceiling. "Why?"

Mary shifted herself forward on the piano bench so she could lean back a little without touching the keys. "Better conversation. Better quality of conversation. When we're all together, each person wants to talk about what she's been up to, but because there are four of us, each has less time. And that's all we talk about then. Getting caught up. It's surfacy, there's no depth to the discussion." Mary raised the right side of her lips, the way Mel might have. "And sometimes one doesn't want to say in front of the others what she'd feel comfortable saying only to me."

"Are you the person they bring their problems to?" the second judge asked.

"I wouldn't say 'problems,' no, but sometimes. Me or Leila."

"Do you play cards, Mary?" the third judge asked, shifting his weight to the left.

"Not usually, no."

"Because in cards, spades is the highest suit, followed by hearts, diamonds, and clubs, which is the lowest suit. A lot of people don't know that. So you could consider yourself a spade, Leila a heart, Lizzy a diamond, and Julietta a club. From what we've observed."

"Julietta is a nice girl," Mary said defensively.

"No one is saying otherwise," the second judge said, parting his hands.

"Next slide please, Mr. Slide-Advancer," the first judge said, moving his head back so he could stare at the screen.

And there was a picture of Rhoda, Fred, Wally, and Gerald, with Shelley the Dancing Crab in her tub.

"Too bad this isn't animated," the third judge said, and clasped his hands in front of him. To Mary, that suggested eagerness.

"Did you enjoy it?" the first judge asked.

"More than I expected to," Mary said.

"Why didn't you expect to?" the first judge asked, leaning back again, which made his question sound less pressing.

"It was different. Not what I'm used to."

"Does that make it bad?" the second judge asked.

"Not necessarily," Mary said, but they could tell she was uncomfortable. Then she laughed to relieve some of the tension. "Leila said the woman was a floozy. I like that term; I hadn't heard it in a long time."

"Old terms can be very reassuring," the second judge said, and rested his right hand in his lap.

"Next slide please, Mr. Slide-Advancer." But as soon as the next slide appeared, the first judge yelled "Next!"

And Mary had never heard any of them raise their voices. "What did I miss?" she asked.

"We'll get back to it," the first judge said, sounding composed again. "Surely you remember this man."

And there was the nameless man taunting Mary. Because of the angle at which the picture was taken—and let's be honest, it had to have been taken by someone—Mary didn't appear in it.

She swallowed loudly and stiffened. "Yes. I remember him."

"Okay," the first judge said. "Previous slide, please, Mr. Slide-Rewinder," and the other two judges laughed.

It was a closeup of the nameless man, his face filling almost the entire screen. His head was tilted down slightly, his eyes squinted, and his mouth was set indifferently. He was neither frowning nor smiling. The background was deep red, almost maroon, and on a flat surface—it must have been a table or a desk—was a long, thin knife that caught the light in such a way as to make it appear gleamingly polished. It might almost have been an advertisement.

"Mary," the first judge said. "He had that with him. He could have killed you. Lizzy was right."

Mary thought she was going to cry. "Why didn't he, then?" she asked.

"Because you were lucky," the third judge said.

"Because you were blessed," the second judge said.

"Because he didn't need to," the first judge said.

And Mary asked, "What would have forced him to the point of need?"

"Threat," the second judge said. "You didn't threaten him enough."

Quickly the third judge held up his right hand and said, "Please understand what we mean by that. We're not saying that you should have threatened him with anything, but that you didn't threaten him enough. We're saying that your being Chinese, your being Indian, and your being a woman wasn't quite enough to push him over the edge. At least not that time."

"Where is he now?" Mary asked.

"We don't know," the first judge said, but with such a lack of inflection that Mary couldn't tell whether he was relieved by that or regretted it.

But then something occurred to Mary. "Where was that picture taken?" she asked.

"In his home," the first judge said.

"It was posed," the third judge said.

"Where does he live?" Mary asked.

"Not around here," the first judge said.

Then she yelled at them. "Game time is over! Why won't you tell me?!"

"Because we don't know," the second judge said calmly.

"The picture was posed," the third judge said.

Mary took a deep breath when she saw her vision starting to blacken. What really scared her wasn't the picture of the man or the knife or not knowing where it came from. What scared her was the picture showing something she couldn't have seen—the inside of the man's house—just like, she remembered, the picture of Ken and Ellora sitting at his kitchen table. She'd never seen that, either, and if the judges really were an extension of her, they couldn't have seen anything she hadn't, or been anywhere she wasn't. And if they were an extension of her, why couldn't she perform their parlor tricks, as she liked to think of them, like making the projector and screen appear and disappear and turning the light out? Maybe she had it all wrong. Or maybe she was just underestimating herself.

She stood up, adjusted her skirt, walked to the recliner, looked outside, then walked back to the piano bench and took a deep breath. "Okay," she said. "Now I have some questions for you." Her lips flattened temporarily. Then, more comfortably, "And a few comments I'd like to make."

"Fair enough," the first judge said, and moved his head slightly forward. "The slide show is over." And, once more, the brass lamp on the drum table illuminated and the projector and screen disappeared. "But first, of course, an announcement."

And Mary half-expected them to announce that now that she understood who they were, they'd be leaving.

But instead the first judge said, crossing his feet, "We've made our judgment wholly in your favor. But let me explain why."

"Of course," Mary said, but to her their announcement sounded rushed. She could tell they were uncomfortable. "No arguments against?" she asked.

"No arguments against," the first judge said, shaking his head.

"No exhibit A?"

The third judge laughed. "Not even an exhibit A."

"In the first place," the second judge said, "you handled your friend Julietta well. Extremely well."

Mary rolled her eyes and laughed. "Yes, not Julietta. *My friend* Julietta."

"She admires you and likes you more than you think," the first judge said.

"I'm sure she does," Mary said, looking startled, then smiling. "She just doesn't know how to show it. Like my mother. That's okay. After a while you get used to people like that showing things in their own way. You don't wait for what's conventionally appropriate."

"Exactly!" the third judge said, suddenly leaning forward.

"And the nameless man," the first judge said, perhaps too solemnly, Mary thought, because she could no longer see him as a threat.

"Yes?" Mary asked, turning to look behind her.

"Do you think you would have reacted differently if you knew he had a knife on him?" the second judge asked, resting his left arm along the backrest.

Mary put on a faux-surprised expression and said, "I'm not sure. Because when he threatened me, when he said whatever he said about cutting my ugly throat, I was pretty sure he had a knife with him. I just couldn't believe he would use it in front of so many people."

"Probably not," the third judge said.

"And there were police around," the second judge said.

"So why didn't they do anything?" Mary asked.

The second judge shook his head. "They weren't standing around you."

"But the real reason we find in your favor," the first judge said, extending his arms and leaning forward, "or, rather, the reason that we find most compelling to influence a favorable decision, is that you found comfort in yourself."

"Comfort and peace," the second judge said.

Mary looked confused. "Meaning what?"

"Meaning," the second judge said, leaning back far enough to lift his feet off the floor, "that you didn't compromise yourself at all today. You were perfectly supportive of Julietta without sacrificing your patience, your time, or your integrity."

"Well done," the third judge said.

"And as regards the nameless man, as you call him," the first judge said, "even though he was a threat—"

"No," the second judge said. "Even though he *thought* he was a threat—"

"You didn't let yourself get hurt by him. Physically or mentally."

"Maybe a little," Mary said, smiling the way she always would when she was embarrassed by praise.

"You should celebrate yourself for that," the second judge said, leaning back and stretching.

"It's not because I ignored him," Mary said. "Some people might think I did."

"Who?" the first judge asked.

"I just—"

"Just what?" the second judge asked, leaning forward.

But Mary didn't know what to say. *Thought I was more important than him?* Trite. *Knew he couldn't hurt me?* Inaccurate. *Had better things on my mind?* Untrue. So she said nothing.

"You're not used to attacks like that," the first judge said. "You're lucky."

Mary lowered her head. "I keep to myself," she said. "But sometimes I get attacked for that, too."

"Though," the second judge said, raising his right arm, then hesitating. "Though it can teach you a lot about yourself and the world around you. If you know what to pay attention to."

For a moment, then, the judges were silent, before the first judge said, "Now you said there were things you wanted to talk to us about."

Mary had a queasy expression on her face. "There are, and I do," she said. She breathed in deeply. "I think, finally, I understand you now." She had to say "I think," because she wasn't sure that she did understand them, in the sense of knowing who they were, and she didn't want to sound pretentious. Pretense, she thought, could anger the judges. In fact, she'd originally wanted to say, "I know who you are now," but that would have sounded threatening. How sad, she thought, that recognizing something could be threatening.

"Well, we're glad to hear that," the first judge said, raising his hands slightly from his legs, but Mary found the response disappointing. She was hoping for a more emphatic reaction. Maybe they weren't impressed, or maybe they were just playing games with her. Or maybe, of course, she was wrong.

"Understanding is always good," the second judge said, "even when we understand something we don't want to."

What did he mean by that? Why would she not want to understand it? Would her realization ultimately hurt her? So she said, "But I'd like to ask you a question. A direct question. If you don't mind."

"Of course," the first judge said, sitting back.

"Why don't you sound like me?"

For a moment there was silence, as Mary knew there would be, and then she was sure she'd asked them something they didn't want to answer, because, she thought, they liked keeping their secrets to themselves, just the way she did.

But then the first judge laughed; not heartily, but enough to let Mary hear it, after which the second judge laughed, a little louder, and then the third judge laughed, too.

"It's all good-natured, Mary. Surely you understand that," the second judge said. He was referring to their laughter.

The first judge shook his head. "The reason we don't sound like you is that nobody knows how she sounds to someone else, does she?"

"No," Mary said, "of course not." That was true, but was the first judge's statement an affirmative answer, telling her that yes, she was right, they were an extension of her, or was it simply a statement of fact?

She no longer knew if she was right and, given the thought that being right might lead to difficulties and complications, was no longer sure that she wanted to be. But to save face, she said, "But here's something I do know. And I'm sure I'm right about this. I know that you're not three people; you're a single person."

"Mary," the first judge said.

"Mary," the second judge said.

"Mary," the third judge said. All with the same voice, as always, but all with the same inflection, not as always.

"You're not stupid," the first judge said. "You're a bright woman."

"Or something in between," the third judge said, raising the index finger of his right hand, "like most people are."

"In the first place," the first judge said, "we're not people, and you know that. Have you ever seen people who look like us?"

"Of course not," the second judge said, laying his palms facedown on his knees and leaning forward. "We're...how can we describe ourselves?"

"Aspects," the third judge said. "Facets."

"Yes, facets. Excellent!" the second judge said, and the first judge nodded.

"We're different facets of a single personality," the first judge said. "People's personalities aren't so one-dimensional that everybody acts in only a certain way."

"At least not normally," the third judge said.

"They have different facets. But whether that combination of facets makes us," the first judge said, and pointed to the three of them in turn, "a single entity or different entities is up to you to decide. We know you've thought about that lately. Why not think about it some more, knowing what you know now?"

"No," said the third judge, shaking his head. "She's recognized that all along."

The second judge reached his left hand back to scratch his neck. "But she hasn't always admitted it to herself," he said.

The third judge laughed. "And if you don't, you're being just as prejudiced as we are." And after a moment he said, "And don't worry, that's a joke."

"Mary," the first judge said, people are made up of an infinite number of facets. Some are similar between people, others are different between people. Very often, maybe more often than not, people are attracted to, or feel more comfortable with, other people who display the same facets or, as you would say, 'have beliefs and interests in common.' Which is all well and good. Except that it overlooks the innate complexity of human beings. Sometimes the unmatching facets they show are going to outnumber the matching ones, and one or the other person involved is going to feel betrayed. Or, to phrase it in the vernacular, people see aspects of others' personalities that they'd rather not see. You've overcome that largely because you stick to yourself and your interests are limited. As a result, there's very little for other people to find out about you beyond what you show them."

"Which is wonderful for someone like you," the third judge said, "because it keeps others from digging too deeply."

"It's honest," the second judge said, nodding. "You have less to hide than most people do."

And Mary smiled at the judges, relishing the irony.

"But then a facet that you'd rather not see comes out," the third judge said. "And when that happens, particularly to someone as focused as you are, you start to fragment."

"And that's how you end up with us," the first judge said.

Which may have been a tacit confession that she'd been right all along, that they were only aspects or facets of her personality, but she couldn't ask them about that outright because, as I said, she didn't want to find out she was wrong. With time, she would learn not to ask. With time, she would have no reason to ask.

"This is a good conversation," the second judge said.

"We're enjoying ourselves," the third judge said. "Are you?"

Mary shook her head but smiled. "Just one more question before you go," she said.

"Of course," the first judge said.

"The picture of the nameless man, that was taken in his house. Who took it?"

"We don't know," the first judge said.

"It wasn't us," the second judge said.

"Evidence, if you want to call it that," said the first judge, "is handed to us, and we use that as the basis of our decisions. But we never question its provenance."

So if the judges weren't taking their own pictures, Mary thought, they could still be an extension of her, because they weren't seeing things she couldn't. Though she had no idea how they got them. Guardedly she said, "All right. I think I feel better now."

"I'm glad," the first judge said. "Then it's time for us to say goodbye."

"Goodbye," the second judge said, and nodded.

"Goodbye," the third judge said, and cleared his throat. He might have added "For now," but he didn't.

And with the judges withdrawing into silence and immobility, Mary walked back into the kitchen to finish the salad she'd just nibbled at before, and drink not another glass of tomato juice but the iced tea she'd shared with Leila, Lizzy, and Julietta.

After a time she got into bed and, as she'd promised herself, listened to her recording of the Brahms First Violin Sonata, the one that always brought back memories of her first Thanksgiving weekend that she was in college, when she spent time again with her friends from high school. And, as she always did, she thought about them but, as she never would, she didn't miss them, because there was no reason to. People don't miss the good times they had, they miss the lost opportunities to make something good to begin with. How she would look back on the day that was just closing, she didn't know. Maybe some day some other piece of music would let her return to it and relive it, in her memory, without any flaws, and that, at least, was something to look forward to.

So she went to sleep that night feeling happy, knowing, or almost knowing, or thinking she knew, that by the morning the judges would be gone. If they weren't, that would mean that she'd been wrong, and they weren't who she believed they were. But she couldn't imagine that happening.

nd yet, it did happen. The judges were still there the next morning, the next afternoon, the next evening, and for many years to come. Did that mean Mary didn't realize who they were? I can't answer that, not because I don't know, but because it's the wrong question to ask. The judges wouldn't leave when Mary recognized them, they would leave when Mary didn't need them anymore, and that couldn't happen until she realized what she was capable of and understood how much power she had. And that, as we all know, takes time. Besides, the longer they stayed, turning into habit, the less she wanted to see them go. Which, ironically, had not been the judges' intention at all. So, for years, the same pattern of incidents followed: she would do something, she would be judged, sometimes she would be remembered and sometimes she would be forgotten, and sometimes she liked being remembered and sometimes she preferred being forgotten.

But then one day the judges did, in fact, leave, never, as they say, to be seen or heard from again. For the longest time Mary looked for them because, while they were there, they never really disappeared; they could always be counted on to be sitting on her couch, and she got used to them. So when, one morning, she walked into her living room and didn't see them, she had a feeling that they might never return, and she was right. But the thought obsessed her that one day they would come back, and she worried over that until there was no more reason or time left to worry.

INTERVIEWER: What's your favorite ending to a piece of classical music? But let's make it a quiet ending, because there are too many loud ones. To choose from, I mean.

MARY: And there are more quiet endings than you might think, so I don't know.

INTERVIEWER: Oh, I bet you do.

MARY (*Laughs*): Oh, I bet I do, too, but it depends on when you ask me. Ask me that question tomorrow, *and I'm just speaking theoretically*, and I might have a different answer. But for now I'm going to stick with "I don't know," because I don't want to commit myself. That said, there are two endings that stand out. Neither is a favorite, exactly, but they haunt me in different ways.

INTERVIEWER: Okay.

MARY: First is the quiet ending that nobody thinks of as "quiet"; the ending to Dvořák's *New World Symphony*. The orchestra rouses itself, hammers out its final chords, in the major key, no less, so happily and resolutely, and then, suddenly, the last chord goes dead. It's very disturbing. It doesn't strike me as content or sad or bittersweet or nostalgic; I don't know what the composer was aiming for, but I find it disturbing. My other quiet ending of note is the ending to Tchaikovsky's *Pathétique*; very famous. Though it took me years to realize that, when you hear the ending, it puts the rest of the symphony into perspective. It's not about loss, it's not about sadness, it's not about suffering. It's about emotional emptiness. Numbness. What follows loss and sadness and suffering. The sadness is over and you've finally gotten rid of it, yes, but you've also gotten rid of everything else. So nothing is left. It's one of the great endings in classical music. *I* think. But you want to know something? You can't talk about only pieces with quiet endings.

INTERVIEWER: Why is that?

MARY: Because they *all* end quietly. A piece of music isn't over until the last sound dies away.

To her credit, if you could call it that, Mary never mentioned the judges to anybody, not even at the end. Certainly nobody was going to believe her, and she didn't want to be locked up as a lunatic. And how they left Mary, which is to say, remembered or forgotten, is up to the reader to decide, but I think the perceptive among us will know exactly how things turned out, so I will say only this: in the end, everything resolved itself favorably and well.

For her.

For Mary.

Mary Sorabi.

Who?

ACKNOWLEDGMENTS

My sincerest thanks to PP-E for his fascinating and brilliant designs, and a special secret thank you to IK for showing me how to begin.

Lightning Source UK Ltd.
Milton Keynes UK
UKHW012006240123
415916UK00016B/241/J